GUAVAS THE TINNER

HE SAW STANDING BEFORE HIM THE FIGURE OF A WOMAN IN A DARK MANTLE.

Page 9.

GUAVAS THE TINNER

BY

S. BARING-GOULD

WITH ILLUSTRATIONS BY FRANK DADD

PHILADELPHIA:

J. B. LIPPINCOTT COMPANY.

1897.

To my Friend

ROBERT BURNARD, Esq., J.P.

MY FELLOW-WORKER IN

EXCAVATING PREHISTORIC VILLAGES, AND THE

BLOWING HOUSES OF OLD TIN-WORKERS

ON DARTMOOR.

IN REMEMBRANCE OF

MANY HAPPY DAYS SPENT TOGETHER.

CONTENTS

CONTENTS

LIST OF ILLUSTRATIONS

GUAVAS THE TINNER

CHAPTER I

SEMI-CRUCIFIED

THE moon glared from the sky, white, hard, with a remorselessness in its light, that brought out into hideousness all that was hideous, and flung inky shadows that were themselves full of horror. Dense clouds lumbered across the sky, stood like a frowning brow above the staring eye, then covered it like a falling lid, and all was darkness, save where, far away, a moorland sweep or a granite pile caught the light, and shone ghostlike in the midst of prevailing darkness.

A wind, cutting as a knife, chilling as an icicle, moaned over the moors, sobbed around the masses of rock, and hissed in the wiry grass and rushes.

Fastened to a stout oak beam, that was planted deep in the soil and wedged with stones, was a young man without jerkin, in his coarse linen shirt, the sleeve of the left arm rolled back to the shoulder, and the left hand attached above his head to the post by a knife, driven through his palm.

His right hand was bound behind his back. About his feet leaped a huge wolf, now howling, then fawning on him, now endeavouring to scramble up him, then stationary, snuffing the air.

The wolf smelt blood.

It smelt the blood that oozed round the knife and ran down the arm of the semi-crucified man.

He knew this. He knew that if the wolf tasted his blood, all the ties that had attached the beast to him would be rent and forgotten, that it would fly at his throat and tear him who had reared it and divided his every meal with it.

Therefore, as the man was powerless to defend himself, save with his feet, he constantly wiped the rill of descending blood with his beard and head of hair, lest it should run within reach of the brute.

" Off Loup ! Keep distance ! " he ordered, and with his foot thrust the beast away.

The wolf obeyed momentarily, then ran in a

circle round the post, with nose in the air, snuffing, then returned to the man, leaped from behind, and endeavoured to lick his arm.

The moon had been behind a cloud, but along the horizon had been drawn a thread of ashen white light, like the edge of a breaker. This was a chain of moorland to the east, on which the rays of the moon fell.

Now the orb broke into full effulgence ; it seemed to tear its way through the vapours with savagery and impatience, as of a caged beast of prey, or as if it were hungering to have another good stare at the tortured man, knifed to a post and exposed to the wolf.

As it burst out from the cloud, its intensity of light dazzled the sufferer, fevered with pain. He turned his head away, and leaned his cheek against the post to which he was fastened. He thought — but this was fancy, that the moon laughed at what it gazed upon. It had looked on many horrors in the lapse of ages through which it had revolved in heaven, and always with the same callousness, never with a flush of indignation at human wantonness and wickedness in the dealings of man with brother man.

The moon now revealed his features as he leaned his head against the post.

The man was comparatively young — about

thirty-four; he had thick dark hair, a dark beard and heavy eyebrows, a keen-cut profile, with splendidly moulded nose, and finely shaped lips. He was muscular, tall, and well built.

And now one terrible consequence of his situation ensued. Cramp came into the extended arm, and the muscles were knotted into huge lumps. The sweat of agony broke out over his face; his eyes, his teeth gleamed in the moonlight, and a gasp of pain escaped from his throat.

He leaped to ease the tension on the strained nerves, and the wolf barked and leaped as well.

But who was this man crucified to a post in mid moor, and wherefore did he thus suffer?

The man was Eldad Guavas, a tinner, and he suffered by sentence of the Bargmaster of the Stannaries, because he had found gold and had appropriated it; whereas gold was due to the Crown.

The time of the story is the reign of Queen Elizabeth, and the scene is Dartmoor.

A few words must be devoted to the tinning on the Duchy of Cornwall estates, and to the penalties inflicted by the Stannary Court for breach of its laws.

We need not go back to the remote period before the Roman conquest of Britain for the beginning of the tin industry in the west of our island, although undoubtedly thence most of the tin was drawn which was employed for the manufacture of bronze in Europe, and to some extent in Asia. It will be sufficient for our purpose briefly to sketch the history of the tin mining during the last three centuries of the Middle Ages.

In the reign of Edward I., in 1288, a series of Stannary Laws were promulgated. Over the Duchy a bailiff, or Bargmaster, was appointed, and every miner was allowed two "meeres" of land in which to work. Each meere consisted of ninety-six square feet. But along with this portion went another meere, which belonged to the Crown, and of all the ore raised a thirteenth portion was due to the King. A miner who left his claim unworked for three weeks lost his right to it. One who was convicted of theft of ore from a neighbour's claim was mulcted in money. If he was again convicted he underwent a heavier sentence, but for a third he was condemned to have his hand affixed to a post at his workings by a knife thrust through the palm, and he was to be left thus affixed to die of hunger, unless he chose to tear himself loose; but this could be done only by cutting through the tendons of his hand, and rendering it for ever useless.

The King claimed one-thirteenth of all tin raised, and demanded the whole of the gold that was found along with the tin, and, as the crime of stealing from the Crown was three times as grave as stealing from an ordinary miner, such a crime could only be expiated by fastening the hand by means of a knife to the post, with the consequence of death or mutilation.

The tin and gold lie almost pure on the surface in every dip and valley, and this is called stream tin or stream gold, and is distinct from the metal extracted by mining in the solid rock.

In early days only stream tin and gold were collected, but when the supply of surface metal was exhausted miners began to burrow under ground and follow the veins or lodes.

Of gold very little was found, and what was found the miners were bound to surrender to the lord of the manor, and the lord of the manor of the Duchy, whether in Devon or Cornwall, was the Crown or Plume of Feathers.

It was, however, extremely difficult to enforce this rule. The miners put the gold they collected in goose quills, easily concealable, and disposed of it to Jews who prowled about among the mining settlements, or to goldsmiths in the towns adjoining the moors.

As the need, or the greed, of the Crown increased, the charges on the miners became more onerous. They were required to surrender one-tenth, and then one-eighth of the ore, and further to bring all their metal to one of the Stannary towns, there to be stamped, and to pay a fee for the stamping. Eventually the claim of the Crown amounted to the equivalent of one-thirteenth of the raw produce.

As more was exacted from the miner, greater was his inducement to evade payment ; accordingly the penalties were accentuated. A miner who defrauded the revenue of ore to the value of thirteenpence halfpenny forfeited his claim, his house, and all his possessions ; he was expelled from the Guild of Tinners, and no man might take him into his service under pain of forfeiture of all his goods.

It is commonly supposed that the last wolf in England was killed in the reign of Edgar, but this is not what the chronicler, William of Mal-mesbury, states. He merely says that Edgar com-manded Judwall, King of the Welsh, to pay him yearly a tribute of three hundred wolves, and that this the Welsh prince continued to do for three years, after which he declared that he could find no more. The statement refers to Wales only, and, as a matter of fact, wolves remained on Dartmoor and Exmoor till the reign of the Tudor sovereigns. Probably the last she-wolf had been hunted down a few years before the opening of this story, when all her cubs were killed with the exception of one, which was secured by the tinner, Eldad Guavas, and was brought up and domesticated by him.

Eldad had been convicted before the Bargmaster of having disposed of gold from his diggings, and after a summary trial the sentence had been executed.

And now Eldad stood knifed through his left hand, writhing with cramp, with teeth set and the breath blowing through his nostrils in puffs of steam, and forced to turn his head from the glare of the cruel moon.

He had to make his selection—to tear away his hand, when the tendons would be cut through, and his fingers fall apart, never more to be used, or to remain with the chance of disengaging his other hand so as to be able to reach and pluck forth the knife. This was what he had hoped to do, and he had worked the rope that bound his arm against the post, in the expectation of being able in time to fret the strands to such an extent that with a wrench he might liberate the hand, and then one hand would free the other.

But the cramp setting in, knotted up his

muscles and concentrated his agony and rendered it acute ; together with this torture came now into his heart the fear lest the wolf, rendered uneasy by the smell of blood, should forget its obligations to him, and fly at his throat. He began to despair of escape in any other way than the first.

"God help me !" he cried, "it must be so !"

But just as he was resolved to release his left hand, he saw standing before him in the moonlight the figure of a woman in a dark mantle wrapped around her.

CHAPTER II

ISOLT

" FOR God's sake—whoever you are—help !
help ! "

The agonised man had bitten at the post in his
pain and torn away a mouthful of wood fibres.
These he spat forth before he could speak, and
now again the horrible cramp was on him, and
he twisted as a wounded worm. Not only were
the muscles of the extended arm knotted up, but his
entire frame seemed to be drawn into a contracted
lump about the post.

The woman drew near, wrapping her black
cloak closer around her, covering her arms,
exposing only her white face and her feet.

She watched the writhing man till the convul-
sion was passed, and then, as he turned his sweat-
bathed face to her, unable to speak through
exhaustion, but moving his lips in entreaty, she
said : " I am ready to help—on one condition."

He bent his head and opened his lips.

"If I release your hand—give it me, to do therewith what I will."

"It is yours."

Leisurely, with firm tread, she stepped to his hut, near the door of which he was crucified, removed a low stool from its place—the stool on which he was wont to sit at the fall of eve, when work was over, or when waiting till his furnace was glowing; and this stool she brought to the post, mounted on it, and laid hold of the haft of the knife.

The wolf sprang up, and would have stood as well on the stool; but she spurned the beast from her; and now her black mantle fell back and exposed her ivory arms.

The knife was so firmly driven into the post that she had to use much exertion to withdraw it, and in so doing even to widen the wound in the man's palm. Finally, she drew the knife forth, and the limb fell to his side.

Instantly the wolf sprang at the blood-stained hand—the hand that had fed it; and had not the woman leaped from the stool and struck at the wolf with the knife, driving the beast into retreat, it would have torn its master in hot craving for blood.

Eldad Guavas stood leaning against the post to

which he had been fastened, with the moon full on his face. The relief he felt made him tremble in all his limbs, and his teeth to chatter. This was the reaction after the tension to which every muscle had been exposed. In this condition he could not speak.

Then the woman laid hold of him, putting her right arm around him, and slowly conducted him to the hut.

"Sit there," she said, and pointed to a stone. "Rest, and hold up thy hand lest that wolf attack thee again."

The tinner obeyed in silence. He raised both his hands to cover his face, leaning the elbows on his knees. He sobbed as a child, and was ashamed that it should be known. He covered his face that his unmanliness might not be observed. But in very truth there was nothing unmanly in his tears; they broke from his eyes, and the sobs from his breast, as involuntarily as did the sweat from his pores and the blood from his veins.

Then the woman went into the hut, and, kneeling, endeavoured to blow the embers on the hearth into a glow. The embers were those of turf, which retains the fire for many hours, and with a little patience an apparently extinct mass of ashes may be quickened to life again. But this woman had not the patience to blow with her lungs, or else she knew of a better method. She pulled a leather strap, then there sounded a rush of water, the creak of a wheel, and next the sigh of indrawn air through the valves of a bellows, followed by a blast of wind.

In another moment she had turned the nozzle of the bellows to the hearth, and the current of air was driven among the light ashes, sending them flying in a cloud, but speedily directing and concentrating its force on a spark that grew in volume to a ruddy disc of fire.

The man was glad that he was alone in the fit of weakness that had come upon him.

The scene was strangely weird and picturesque. A little above where he sat, the river Yealm broke over a barrier of granite in a cascade commonly known as The Steps. The fall is about forty feet, but the water is not in all places visible, as here and there it dives under a mass of fallen rock, whereas in other places it dances in a glittering sheet over a granite lip.

The Yealm having descended the Steps, races away in a glen between boulder-strewn moorland slopes : and at the bottom of the Steps, on a little patch of gravel round which swept the river, the hut and blowing house of Guavas were planted.

The river leaping from its moorland cradle

might have been one of pure moonlight, or molten
tin as it issues from the furnace. The tinner's
dwelling was an oblong construction, rectangular,
consisting of two chambers, or, to be more exact,
of two hovels that adjoined, with a narrow communication between them.

The doorway was formed of unshaped blocks
of granite, with a lintel as rude, above; and the
single window that lighted the dwelling-house
was of equally primitive construction. It had no
framework of wood set in the opening, and no
glazing. It was not more than a foot in height,
and when Guavas desired to shut out the cold, he
closed it with a sheep-skin stretched across the
opening from pegs. In the dwelling-house a few
boards, covered with moss and heather, formed a
seat by day and a bed by night. There was no
table in the place, only one stool. The furnace
in which the tin was melted was in the same
apartment, and formed a portion of the hearth,
which latter was composed of flat, fine grained
elvan. The smelting furnace was built up of
granite lined and coated with clay, with a chimney
carried through the wall to the open air, whereas
the smoke from the hearth rose and forced its
way out at window or door, without provision
made for its exit through the roof.

Adjoining the chamber was a store-house, in

which the mining tools were preserved, where was the oak chest that contained Guavas' best clothes and linen ; there also was kept his unstamped tin. This latter, his most precious commodity, was concealed in a recess in the wall of the store-house, a cave dug out of the bank of the hill against which the habitation leaned, and the entrance to it was disguised by wall-stones laid in courses fitting the opening.

From a streamlet that is a confluent of the Yealm, a leat or watercourse had been conducted at a slight incline to the small water-wheel, but six feet in diameter, that worked the bellows employed for maintaining a blast in the furnace. The methods adopted at the period of this story for the mining and the smelting of the tin were as rude as any employed by savages, and yet it was in advance of those adopted by the first tinners at the dawn of the Middle Ages.

The western stream tin is pure. It can be run out of the ore in an ordinary peat fire. Indeed, in places where the peat itself is full of granite granules, a fire will leave on the hearth a globule of tin that has been extracted by the heat without a blast.

The bellows employed in the early Middle Ages had been of the rudest description, consisting of boxes with skins stretched over them, which could be raised or depressed by the hand so as to cause an artificial draught. But of recent years the water-wheel had been introduced, and an immense stride forward had been taken. Now the water itself worked the bellows and created the blast. But the mining was still in a primitive condition. Shafts and adits were sunk and run, but to no great depth, and only when a party of miners agreed to work together as a company. Usually they preferred to act independently of each other.

The earliest tin workings had been in the streams, without mining at all, and this was still the general practice. Nevertheless great works, signs of mining, properly so-called, remained, and were attributed, traditionally and inaccurately, to the Romans.

Eldad had time to recover himself in the fanning air and the soft moonlight, with the rush of the stream in his ear and the molten silver glinting at his feet—all soothing influences.

His heart beat more evenly, his muscles resumed their wonted flexibility, and his breath came and went more regularly.

When the woman issued from the hut she found him seated with the wounded hand thrust into the bosom of his shirt, the other leaning over his knee ; his face was calm, and when he spoke his voice was composed. He looked steadily and curiously at her, and said :

"Isolt Rodda."

"Aye, that is I," answered she, and stood still.

She was tall—in the moonlight could be seen how handsome she was, with features inclined to harshness, her profuse dark hair, like pitch, poured over her head and shoulders, her dark brows arched, and casting deep shadows under them.

"It is *you* who have released me ?"

"It is I."

"And your father sentenced me."

"It was so."

He was embarrassed. He desired to ask questions, yet found a difficulty in framing them. She observed this.

"Come," she said, "the time for explanation is not arrived. First thy hand must be bound up. Hast thou oil in thy house ?"

"Aye, there be both wax and oil ; you will find them in the store-chamber."

"That is well. I will mix them and bind up thy hand with them, and after that I will tell thee all." .

She retired to the hovel, kindled a rushlight, and after some search found what was required. She proceeded to dissolve the wax in a stone frying-pan,[1] mixed it with oil, and then poured the melted matter on a linen rag; after which she came forth to Eldad. She first thoroughly washed the wound with the pure water that foamed over the steps, and then dexterously applied the plaster and bound up the hand.

When this was done Isolt seated herself on a stone over against Eldad, but so that her face was in shadow.

"I will tell thee why I have done it," she said, "and spare the labour of questioning. It is true that my father, the Bargmaster, condemned you to be knifed for stealing gold that belongs to the Queen; but my father had no right to thus sentence you. He had no right to do other than send you to Lydford Castle, there to be tried, or there to be kept till such time as you were properly tried. But he was in a hurry, he and Dickon Rawle, and the times are unsettled, and he thought no inquiry would be made."

Guavas moved his uninjured hand to arrest her in what she was saying, that he might interject a question. She observed his motion, and said:—

"I know what you would ask. Listen and you shall hear all. But first I demand whether thou

[1] Stone frying-pans found among stream works in Cornwall and Devon are made of a volcanic stone that stands the fire.

rememberest and wilt observe the condition on which I set thee free ?"

Eldad bent his head.

"That is not sufficient," said Isolt. "Raise thy hand to the stars, and swear that thou wilt observe it, or that every blight and blast and curse wherewith in the old religion men were withered may fall on thee."

"You asked me to surrender to you the hand you released," said Eldad. "It is yours."

"Swear !"

He raised the wounded hand to heaven. "So help me God—unless you again release me."

"So ! you regard yourself as bound—knifed to me by this oath ? And yet you know not what is my purpose with you ?" There were bitterness, scorn, in her tone.

" I am taken by surprise," he explained.

"Oh !" said she, scoffingly, " I ask it in my own and my father's interest, and because I hate Dickon Rawle."

" I have more occasion to hate him than you," said Guavas, gravely. "It was he who got me into my trouble. In very sooth, I had no thought of selling the gold I had found. There were but half a dozen of goose-quills. I thought to have kept them till such time as I should have found a woman to my heart, and then to have made a

ring thereof for her.   But Dickon Rawle came
and over-persuaded me.   There was a Jew, he
said, would pay heavy money for it, and none
would be the wiser.   I held out, but there was
no woman I deemed would have me, for what
woman should I meet up here who would take
a ring from the poor strange miner? . So I
yielded—and that was my ruin."

"Yes," threw in Isolt Rodda, hastily, passion-
ately, "and then Dickon betrayed you, and my
father sentenced you.   He had no right to do it,
and he knew it, but he would be quit of you,
and the other miners were all against you, as a
Cornishman, and would drive you out or kill you
off that you might not be on our moors, and
pitch on our grounds."

" I know that they have looked on me as an
interloper."

"And they have thought to be rid of you by
fair means or by foul."

"Nay, not by fair means, but by foul—foul
only."

"All means are fair in love—and in mining."

CHAPTER III

THE RING

"WELL—and then?" asked Guavas, further. "Dickon Rawle saith that you, the Cornishman, have cut your bounds and made your pitch just under Yealm Steps, and that at the Deluge, when the waters washed away so much of the earth, the tin was carried over the lip and spilled in the largest and purest lumps under the Steps."

"That is not true," said Guavas.

"And that his pitch is above the Steps, whence all the tin was carried away by the retreating waters. Therefore you have his tin as well as your own——"

"Was it his tin when the Deluge swept it down, and the waters retreated from off the face of the earth?"

"He saith that you have all the good and he

all the bad, and he is a man of the place and county, and you are a stranger and a Cornishman. He declareth further that the Bodmin moors and the Liskeard moors are for Cornishmen, and Dartmoor is for the tinners of Devon. He saith, moreover, that it should not be suffered for you to make a pitch and cut bounds where there is most tin of all on Dartmoor; aye, and not tin only, but gold as well. And the other tinners and the spalliers agree with him, and all are united to drive you hence, and Dickon hath set up his rest to unite your claim with his own. To-morrow he will come and cut his bounds where were yours."

"Will he? I shall have something to say to that."

"He will try to do so. How can you prevent him?"

"I have a good friend here," said Guavas, and pointed to the wolf.

"And you have a better friend in me."

"That you have proved yourself to be, Mistress Isolt."

"Dickon has sought to compass the acquisition of your pitch, and the joining it on to his own ever since he found that yours was fat and his was lean. There were men who would have made a company of adventurers with you, but you have stood out against a company, and have worked without a mate."

"That is true."

"All men, therefore, who would have profited by the venture, and greatly desired it, have been set against thee. But it was Dickon who contrived the whole plot, and that I know, for I overheard the contriving thereof. Now that I have thee fast bound to me by solemn oath, I will tell even more. Unto this my father was privy, and he has joined with Dickon, and is to have a share in all ore raised on the Yealm Steps Pitch."

"That is sheer against Stannary Law."

"So was the sentencing of thee. But what care they? Who will interfere? Who will bring the matter before the Warden? And now—now that I have secured you—you, the sufferer, can do so least of all."

Eldad considered a moment, and the muscles of his face worked.

"It is even so," said she. "I have tied you, that you cannot stir against my father; but as for Dickon, do to him, do with him, what you will. Know that it was my father's plan to give me to him. Now, tell me one thing. You said—you were saving the gold you found to make thereof a ring for a woman. For what woman?"

Guavas looked at the strange, dark figure seated

in the moonlight. Isolt's white hands clasped her knee, they alone showed white, all else was dark. She had drawn her cloak as a hood over her face, and had buried it in shadow.

" It was for me ! " she said impatiently.

"Yes, Isolt—that is true. I had seen you. It was I who sang outside your window on May morning, and planted the bush. But I went my way; for I thought—what am I but a poor miner ?"

"A poor miner ! " jeered the girl. "When you have the best pitch on the moor. When the flood of Noah ran away it spilled over the brink of Yealm Steps vast quantities of stream tin and grains of gold mingled with the tin, all—all for thy picking, here on this precious pitch."

"It is true that I have a good piece of ground on which to work. But I am alone."

"Therefore you alone profit thereby. There are not others to divide."

" But the work is the slower."

" Yet it is certain. Nay," said she, unlacing her hands and waving the right, " what is all that to me ? Go on and say what you thought, after that, when you had considered you were a poor miner—poor ! "

" I thought next that you were the Bailiff's daughter, and what was I that I should look so high as to you ? "

"Bah! your fortune is made. It is commonly reported that under the Steps lies a bed of pure stream-tin a man's height, piled up, as thrown over the lip by the Flood."

"That I do not believe."

"Others say it."

"But none have so good knowledge of the pitch as myself. I say it is a good pitch, but not such as you deem."

"You have not worked under the falling water yet?"

"No."

"Then how can you say the bed of tin and gold is not there?"

"How can they say it is there, who have not worked at Yealm Steps at all?"

"Everything is washed away from Dickon's claim above the Steps."

"Who can say there was ever any tin there?"

"Whence comes that you find below?" asked she.

Guavas shrugged his shoulders. "Thou esteemest my claim more highly than it deserves," he said. "Vain are the tales told of its richness; it is a good claim, but nothing marvellous."

"Now," pursued Isolt, "I will show you that I am thankful for the May bush you planted, and that I make one cause with you. To-morrow is the Michaelmas bonding day, and Dickon Rawle will come with his party to cut bonds here, and so drive you from your right. But you must prevent him. You cannot cut turves with your maimed hand. I will do it for you. Where shall I find the shovel ? "

" It stands behind the house," answered the tinner. Then Isolt went to the place indicated, and brought the shovel from it.

Eldad stood up and walked with her to the point where his claim began, it was up the steep slope of the hillside, down which foamed the Yealm in cataract. According to immemorial custom a tinner was required to renew his bounds at Michaelmas every year, under risk of forfeiture.

There were, indeed, mitigations of the penalty, and law was allowed by enactments of the Stannary Court, but Guavas was well aware that he had to do with prejudiced men, judge, jury and all ; and that no scruple would be felt about twisting the law against him, as an intruder.

The Lord High Warden of the Stannaries was a great noble who rarely, if ever, visited the West of England, and looked into the proceedings of his officials. In Cornwall and Devon, at one period, all the tinners had been associated together, and met once a year on Hingeston Hill above the Tamar, to settle their differences; but these differences, instead of being settled, became aggravated at these meetings, and no accord could be arrived at. There were not only the mutual jealousies of workers in rival tin-regions with the fluctuations of yield in each, but also through the middle ages the miners of Cornwall and Devon had spoken different languages, and the Cornish tongue was only now beginning to retreat. Differences in language caused the Devon miners to regard the Cornish miners to be different in race, and they assumed a superiority and swagger which were infinitely galling to the sensitive and proud Cornishman. For long Dartmoor had yielded more tin than Cornwall, but now the yield in the former region declined, and the disappointment angered the Devonian workmen and made them resentful against a Cornishman who had dared to " pitch " in the district they claimed as their own. This resentment was aggravated when it was found that he had been extraordinarily lucky in his "pitch."

Now, in the moonlight, Isolt Rodda cut three turves at each angle of the claim of Guavas.

When she had done this, she leaned on the spade.

"Eldad," said she, "I have done for thee what

no other maid has done for other man ; I have done what no maid might do, save for the man who was hers by promise. See that thou be not false to the covenant between us made."

Then Guavas held forth his right hand.

"Isolt," answered he, "it is not the way with Cornishmen to be false. See—on my little finger is a ring. I made it out of gold of my own raising and washing. Take it from my finger. I hold to thee so long as thou holdest the ring. Only when that is parted with are we free the one from the other."

" That is—till death."

" Till death to you or to me."

" It is well," she said ; she plucked the ring from his extended hand and said : " In the name of God—till death."

CHAPTER IV

CROCKERN HALL

ISOLT had vanished into the night, and Guavas was left alone, with the wolf fawning and leaping round him.

" Be still, Loup ! " said he ; then he went to his hut, brought forth a chain, fastened it to the collar of the beast, and attached the end of the chain to the post.

" Be there, and vex me no more," ordered he ; then halting, with his hand against the post, he added : " And yet, poor brute, thou art famished. It is now three days, and thou hast not been fed."

He returned towards the hut to fetch something for the creature, but again halted, this time at the doorway, and mused : " Nay, I may need thee, and thee famished. With thy belly full thou art a sad coward, and dost not answer thy master."

Then Eldad drew the bench away from the post, and placed it where it had been wont to

stand, beside his door. He seated himself thereon, and looked up at the steps with the rippling silver flowing over the rocks, and the stones themselves while in the clear moonlight. His hand pained him greatly, and yet his thoughts were so occupied with what had taken place, and with what might follow thereon, that he had none to spare for his bodily pain.

In the preceding winter, at Christmas, Eldad had met Isolt, the Bargmaster's daughter, for the first time, and that the relation in which these two stood to each other may be understood, as well as her interference for the deliverance of Guavas, it will be necessary at some length, and in some detail, to describe that meeting, although by so doing we are going back to a period antecedent to the opening of this tale.

At the end of the preceding year Guavas had had his mother living with him in the Blowing House Hut ; she was at that time failing in health, and she was since dead.

At Christmas it was usual for the miners and their families to meet for a great common merrymaking in the hall of the Parliament of the Stannary Court at Crockern Tor.

This tor is central in Dartmoor, and annually the Tinners' Parliament, under the Lord Warden of the Stannaries or his deputy, assembled among the rocks on the summit, nearly 1,400 feet above the sea, to transact business. Crockern Tor is by no means one of the highest and boldest heights ; it is perhaps the most insignificant, but on account of its central position and accessibility was from time immemorial the Parliamentary centre of the district. The President occupied a rude stone seat, like a cromlech, and which had probably been in prehistoric times a monument above dead men ; and the jurors and other members of the Court sat about among the granite rocks where they could and would. But as it was by no means uncommon that on the Parliament day a gale would be blowing, and that either fog should envelope the height, or that it should be swept with rain, it was customary, in the event of the weather proving unpropitious, after the formality of the opening of the Parliament, to adjourn to a long, rudely-constructed hall near the road below, where business could be transacted under cover and in comparative comfort.

This hall disappeared when the Parliament was removed in 1749 to Truro, and its site occupied by a coaching inn, when at the close of the century a road was carried across the moor. This still stands, though no longer employed as a tavern.

The great hall, built of masses of granite uncemented with mortar, and thatched with rushes, was the property of the tinners, and was employed by them as a place of gathering for entertainment as well as for business. And of all gatherings for entertainment, none was more looked forward to, and looked back upon, than the Stannary dance in Christmas week.

Sometimes, but not often, snow lay on the moor at that season, and it was a matter of difficulty for the young people of both sexes to make their way to the place of meeting ; but this served to enhance the delight given by the assembly, and the zest with which all who assembled enjoyed themselves.

None appreciated these dances more than the girls, for on the moor men were many and women were few ; nevertheless, a surprising number of maidens did brave the weather, the darkness, and the waste, to meet on such occasions. They came from such villages that surrounded the moor, as were not separated from Crockern Tor by impassable bogs. Possibly one reason why this dance was so frequented by the fair and frail sex, was that at it the matrimonial matches for the year were made. The marriageable tinners then chose who should be their partners for life ; that is, supposing their "pitches" had yielded well during the preceding twelve months, and promised well for those which were coming.

Guavas had not been to these dances. He had no desire to find a mate ; he was not addicted to pleasure. On the day of the dance his mother spoke about it.

" Eldad, you should go to Crockern Tor. All the pretty maids of the country-side will be there, and there be none prettier to be found in all England."

Guavas laughed, and stretching his limbs, and thrusting his hands under his belt, said : " What are the maids to me ? "

" But it is time that thou shouldst concern thyself about them, and choose thee one who will manage thy house for thee."

" Art thou not here, mother ? Do I desire another ? "

" My son, I shall not be here much longer. When I am carried out, then you will be alone, and it is written in Scripture that it is not good for man to be alone."

" There is plenty of time for me to think of that."

" There is not plenty of time, my son. I am fading and falling away. You are not any longer a boy, and man is but young once in his life.'

"We will talk again of this matter a year hence."

"Nay—that may be too late. The pitch is a good one, and the further thou workest the more tin thou findest; therefore I say, get thee a wife. Then will come joy in thy work. If it pleased the Lord that a goodly maid should take thy fancy, I would die happy."

"Speak not of dying, mother."

"Nay—but I must, when I feel the tooth of death gnawing at my heart. A greater joy couldst thou not give me, Eldad, than the thought that when the old leaf falls, a fresh bud were bursting in its place. Go to Crockern Tor, if not because it pleaseth thee, then because it is the desire of thy mother, who will not be on earth to ask of thee favours much longer."

Still Eldad hesitated.

"Tell me, son, hast thou no pleasure in any woman?"

Guavas laughed.

"Mother, thou dost question me like as doth a parson."

The old woman was encouraged by his laugh, and she urged her request. "Go, Eldad, and gratify my heart. Of a surety, no maid would say thee nay. The folk tell of thy pitch and thy finds, and tell more than sooth. See—I have laid out for thee thy Sunday garments. Thou wilt go."

And so, to gratify the old woman, Eldad went.

We must now turn to Crockern Parliament hall, on the evening of the dance.

A great fire of turf warmed the hall, and in part lighted it, but a number of tallow candles in sconces against the walls assisted in illuminating the large space. There was no decoration of ferns and evergreens, as the bracken was dead and there were no evergreens on the moor; all plantations of spruce and Scottish pine now found there, in places, date from the days of the Prince Regent.

The Bargmaster, or Bailiff, was present, a lean man with a stoop in his shoulders and bent head, with a brown face and sharp cunning eyes that were ever on the move, and never met a gaze fully and frankly, but slinked into corners evasively.

Among all the maidens present none approached Isolt in height and presence. They were for the major part fair haired with pure complexions, white and pink, and with soft brown eyes. Only here and there were their orbs blue. The Bargmaster's daughter was tall, with broad but low brow, a dusky complexion, and dark hair. Her features were finely cut, eagle-like, and her eyes as keen and defiant as those of the king of the birds. She held herself erect, and looked round with a contemptuous curl on her thin lips.

The dancing was begun, but Isolt was not forward to dance. Two men sought her favour, the one Richard Rawle, and the other Humphrey Evea. The former was the head of a band of "adventurers" who worked the stream tin on the Yealm, above the Steps. He was more than the captain, he owned land as well in the neighbourhood. The miners at their Court had passed a law which forbade any one to undertake mining and make a claim who owned land above £10 in value, but they were not able to enforce the law, at all events beyond the "Forest" bounds, and the moor through which the Yealm brawled and leaped was not wholly Duchy property, but belonged to the parishioners of Cornwood under the Lord of the Manor. As Rawle's land was in Cornwood, he claimed a right to work for tin upon the common land, and to over-ride the preventive statute passed by the Stannary Parliament.

Rawle was a tall, good-looking man, with very light hair and almost white eyebrows and lashes. The hair of his moustache was straw coloured, and as his face was red with exposure to the wind and sun, the contrast was not to his favour. Had he been a dark haired man he would have been handsome.

The other man, Humphrey Evea, was short dapper, had a merry eye, but somewhat watery. He was no miner, but owned a tenement on the moor which he neglected, because given to drink and idleness. By the grace of God he was both musician and poet, and could improvise verses, not without merit, on any occasion. He was one of those country artists who rises up once in two or three generations, leads a pitiful life, then dies, and leaves behind a heritage of song that remains long after that he, himself, has been forgotten.

" Dance with me," urged Evea, " and I will sing you a song on your beautiful eyes—on your lips that so many would love to touch."

" I would have you sing of anything save me," answered Isolt, shortly.

" Then I'll sing you a song about Dickon Rawle and his neighbour," laughed Humphrey.

" Who is his neighbour ? " asked the girl.

" I forbid you to sing about me," said Rawle, frowning.

There was no love spilled between the two men, each admiring the same woman, and totally opposed to one another in character. Rawle knew that Evea had a biting wit, and that his verses caught the ear and might occasion him unpleasantness.

"Who is Rawle's neighbour?" again asked Isolt.

"He is a Cornishman," answered the lively little man. "I will tell you what he does. He has got a forked ash stick, and he goes about with that, and the stick turns in his hand and points where there is tin—but Dickon, I trow, he has a dousing stick too, but that leads where there is none."

"And so—this Cornishman has pitched well?"

"He has pitched bravely. There is not a better pitch anywhere, and that is not a bowshot off from Dickon's right. Dickon has all the grout and this man all the metal. That makes Dickon mad."

"It is a lie," said Rawle, angrily. "His mother is a witch, and she draws the metal away under ground by means of a magnet the Devil gave her. I can hear it running away as I dig and sift. How can a man fight against devilry?"

"There is no witchcraft in it at all," retorted Evea. "It is all science with the rod. Every Cornishman knows how to use the rod, and that is how this man has the advantage over the Dartmoor miners."

"I say it is devilry; and we will have the old

woman burnt for witchcraft. That Cornish fellow
has found gold as well as silver. And he has a
wolf—savage and strong—to guard his vouga
(hiding-place), where he has the tin ingots heaped
to the top, and the gold in bars."

"How do you know ?" asked Isolt, scornfully.
"Did you brave the savage and strong wolf and
look in ?"

"I have heard say so."

"Who have seen what is cached (hidden) in
the vouga ?"

"It is well known what he has taken to
Plympton Earl to be coined." [1]

"Ah ! then I can understand. But you said
—gold also ?"

"He has gold. He has made himself a ring
of it."

"He is a rich man then ?" said Isolt.

"He is fast becoming one, and drawing away
all the ore from us Devon miners with his hellish
magnet."

"Magnet ! Who has seen it ? What is his
name ?"

"Guavas."

"And what is this fellow like of whom you are

---

[1] No tin might be sold till tested and stamped with the Duchy
arms, at one of the Stannary towns. Moreover, the Crown had
right of pre-emption, as well as toll on the tin raised.

so envious, because he goes up whilst you go down ?"

"Judge for yourself—there he štands."

The door was thrown open, and Eldad stood in it.

CHAPTER V

LINKED FINGERS

WITH roused interest Isolt looked at the tall man who had entered. Guavas stood for a while motionless, till his eyes were accustomed to the light within. Whilst he thus stood, Isolt's orbs were fastened on him. He was taller, more stately in appearance, than any other man in the hall. His face was pale, not ruddy, perhaps by day dusky in hue, now, compared with the red and brown complexions of the fair haired miners of Devon, he looked white. His long raven locks rose off his brow in a wave, and curled behind his ears over his shoulders.

Broad of shoulder, stout of limb, he seemed a greater and a nobler man than every other in the room, as one belonging to a higher caste, shaped in another mould. In type he resembled only herself.   They two belonged to one order, in stature, in colour, in boldness of sculpture of feature.

Slowly Isolt turned her eyes away from the stranger and looked at Evea and then at Rawle, and her beautiful lips curled with contempt. What were these two before the Cornishman ? Were they fashioned out of the same clay ? Were they shaped by the same artist hand ?

Her eyes reverted to Eldad, and now hers encountered his large dark orbs, soft, yet with fire lurking in them.   At once, without knowing why, the blood mounted to her brow and she felt abashed.   She lowered her eyes.

A moment later, and she lifted them again and looked, and again his eyes were fixed on and met hers.   And so it was.   He could not withdraw his eyes from the stately, splendid woman ; and she, on her part, was forced irresistibly to return his glance, and every time that their regards met, her heart leaped.

Then Guavas strode across the space that separated them, and confronting her, said bluntly : "What is thy name ?"

"I am the Bailiff's daughter—I am Isolt Rodda."

Hearing the first words, Humphrey struck up :—

> "There was a youth and a well-beloved youth,
>   And he was a Squire's son ;
> He loved the Bailiff's daughter dear,
>   That lived on Coryndon.
>
> She was coy, and she would not believe
>   That he did love her so ;
> No, nor at any time she would
>   Any countenance to him show."

"Be silent, you fool !" said Rawle. "Isolt, you will dance with me ?"

"Nay, with me," said Evea.

"I will dance with neither," answered the girl, and laid her hand on Guavas' wrist. "Is it not so—you have come to ask me ?"

"I cannot dance," he said.

"And I will not—this time," she said, promptly. "We will speak with each other."

She saw a heavy gold ring on his hand. "That is what you got out of your ground ?" she asked.

"I got it."

"You may keep—but not sell, so I have heard my father say. The gold goes to the Crown."

Eldad laughed. "How much of what is found goes that way ?" he asked.

The fiddler struck up, and the crowd that was in movement and confusion rapidly shaped itself for a country dance, and tongues ceased to wag, as the feet tingled to be in movement.

"You cannot dance ?" queried Isolt.

"No, I cannot dance," he replied.

"Then why did you come hither ? "

"I was drawn—as by a lode-stone."

"By a lode-stone ? "

"By you."

Whilst others danced and the music rang through the hall, these two stood silent, for a while, opposite each other, Isolt with lowered lids. Eldad wondered at the long dark lashes that covered her eyes.

Presently, feeling constrained and feeling also a necessity for breaking through this constraint, he said : "You are fond of dancing ?"

"Aye !   I love it well."

"It grieves me that I cannot dance."

"Oh !" said she, "thou hast other work to do. Dancing befits the others, not thee."

"Why not me ?"

"Because—see—you have also a magnet that draws to thee the precious metals."

"I understand not."

"That is what they say; because you have a good pitch whereas theirs are bad, they say that just as a witch by working the handle of an axe stuck into a beam can milk her neighbour's cows, so canst thou milk the white tin and the red gold out of others' grounds, and draw them to thee."

"That is false. The only magnet I know is not in my possession."

Isolt coloured and looked down abashed.

Then up came Rawle and demanded a dance with the Bargmaster's daughter.

Reluctantly she consented, and allowed him to draw her away.

A shadow came across the brow of Guavas, and his eyes pursued the dancers.

In a country dance the males stand on one side, the females on the other. Whenever the hands of Rawle and Isolt met, the mouth of Guavas worked, and his brows knitted.

It was strange. He had never seen the girl before, nor she him, yet from the moment he entered the hall and their eyes had met, it was as though a spell had been cast on both of them which made them uneasy, nay more, wretched, unless together.

The Bargmaster came to Eldad and spoke to him, but received an answer that showed his mind was distraught.

"That is my daughter," said the Bailiff, "and she hath Dickon Rawle to partner. He hath the grounds that lie above thee on the river. Hast thou any intent to take to thee others on thy claim? Methinks thou couldst not do better than join Rawle to thee, and then thou wilt have a long stretch of river-bed to stream."

"I have no intention to take any to me," answered Eldad, shortly.

" But see how much better thou wouldst work the run. There is no saying but that a man alone may employ his pitch wastefully, and so forfeit his claim. It so stands in the laws."

"Wastefully I shall not work mine," replied Eldad. "Of that be sure; for mine is too valuable to be wasted."

The Bargmaster lowered his voice and said: " It is even to be expected that Richard Rawle will become son-in-law to me. It were not amiss that thou shouldst oblige me. I might help thee in other matters."

"My claim is mine own, and I share with none," answered Eldad, shortly. His heart contracted at the thought that Isolt was to be given to Rawle.

"Thou mayest come to rue this," said the Bailiff; " I gave thee friendly counsel," and turned testily away.

Presently the dance was over, and Rawle took Isolt by the hand to conduct her to a seat at the further end of the hall, but she plucked her fingers away and looked towards Guavas, who at once stepped to her, and she said, "We have not finished that whereof we were speaking."

"And that will engage us the entire evening," he replied.

"As thou dost not dance, thy stay in this place will not be for long," she said.

"I will stay as long as thou dost," he answered, promptly, "or rather, as long as thou dost speak with me. If thou dancest with every Jack and Dickon, I will away."

"I may dance with whom I please," she said, sharply.

Then up came Humphrey Evea to claim her, but unconsciously Eldad laid his hand on her arm to withhold her, and she dismissed the suitor. In like manner she refused all others who sought to draw her into the dance. And when the parties were made up, these two remained alone together once more. They stood opposite each other, and yet conversation would not flow. Eldad was unaccustomed to the society of young girls; to such he knew not what to say. His address resembled the break-up of ice on a river. At first there come down masses of ice, then they meet and bridge the stream and seem to arrest it. In another moment all are in movement and flow again. At first he spoke hesitatingly, awkwardly, about empty nothings, then came to a standstill and he cast about for subjects on which to discourse, then his words flowed with a rush.

Isolt contributed greatly to his relief, for she

turned the current of his thoughts ever in one direction—to the deposit of tin under Yealm Steps, and to the manner in which he had found it.

That he worked the Diviner's rod he did not deny. The faculty to use the hazel twig did not lie in all men; it may have been absent in Dickon Rawle when he made choice of his claim, but in himself the power was unmistakable. It was a heritage from his father and grandfather, who had all been tin streamers. But he laughed when he saw that the girl had formed fantastic and exaggerated notions of the spoil he had got, and was likely to get. His find was good, he added, but not extraordinary.

Isolt accepted this depreciation of his claim as due to caution and cunning, and her conviction that Guavas was in extraordinary luck was not diminished by his disclaimer.

She and the Cornishman paid little or no attention to what passed around them. As they conversed, Eldad linked the little finger of his right hand round the same finger of her left; and through these linked fingers gushed a warm stream from heart to heart, and from brain to brain.

A fire, a dizziness, were in Eldad's head. Was this that he felt love? or was he subject to fascination ? He did not ask himself the question. He did not seek to analyse his feelings. He was lifted into a new and strange atmosphere. He saw, heard, felt, with other senses than those he had exercised heretofore, and his heart beat with new emotions.

"What brought you here this night ?" asked Isolt.

"I have told thee what I believe brought me ; but what sent me forth out of my house, over the moor, was my mother's command."

"She bade thee come ?"

"Aye—even she."

"And wherefore ?"

"That I might see the fair maids."

"Then look about—I am not fair. I am brown ; look not on me."

"Where thou art, I have no eyes for another."

A light pressure from his finger sent a thrill up her arm. Her cheeks darkened with the blood that streamed from her heart, as she saw the gleam in the eyes of Eldad when he spoke.

Her father interposed, caught her by the shoulder, and said :—

"A word with thee, Isolt," and when he had removed her some paces from the Cornishman, he said : "Why art thou standing thus with him —the stranger ? All eyes are on you both, all tongues set a wagging. Are ye bewitched the one and the other? Now, I would have you listen to what Rawle has to say. He has even spoke with me, as there was no getting a word in thy ears, so dulled were they with the talk of the spallier of Yealm Steps."

"What has Rawle to say to me?" asked Isolt, sullenly.

"That I shall answer for myself," said Dickon. "I have come here only to see thee. I have a bit of land of my own, and a pitch above the Steps."

"Which yields nothing," retorted she. "Go thy way till thy claim returns tin, and not grout."

"Then hear me," said Humphrey. "I have no claim at all, but I have a holding on the moor that has supported my ancestors since Adam."

"None will have thee till thou hast learned to respect thyself, Humphrey. As for thy acres, they will go down thy throat in aqua vitæ."

"We are flouted for this Cornishman," exclaimed Rawle, angrily. "With Evea one may contend, but not with one who has a witch for his mother and the devil for his familiar."

At once a blow fell on him from a strong arm, that sent him reeling; he lost his balance and dropped on the floor.

Instantly in at the door leaped the wolf, and sprang on the prostrate man, raised its head and howled.

The music was silenced, the dancers were arrested.

CHAPTER VI

THE SOUL-CAKE

GUAVAS called off the wolf, and Rawle picked himself up. He said no word; he maintained a sullen silence. In the presence of Eldad and his wolf he was afraid to utter the threats that rushed up in his heart.

The Cornishman withdrew. His presence marred the pleasure of the evening and was a menace to its peaceable character. He could not dance; his conversation with Isolt was broken in on by her father, and could not well be resumed. He had no associates, no friends, only enemies in that concourse of merrymakers.

Therefore he left the place, after a look round, and a rest of his eyes on Isolt.

Over bog and moor, hill and dale, Guavas strode on his way home; direct in his course as an arrow, and the wolf trotted at his side. In his right hand he held a staff shod with iron, to serve as a walking-stick or as a defence. Other weapon, save a knife in his girdle, he had none. And, indeed, none was needed on the moors even at that period ; for, although the tinners were capable of high-handed dealings with those who did not belong to the moor, and to their corporation, they maintained strict order throughout the region over which the Stannary jurisdiction prevailed.

A crescent moon was in the sky ; a cold north wind was blowing ; but as Guavas walked due south, it was in his back. Ice and a thin coating of snow lay on the ground, and the ice was sufficiently hard to make the bogs passable, so that he could step along without great concern whether he walked over morass or on solid ground.

Cold though the night was, Guavas felt nothing of the frost and polar blast ; for a fire had been kindled in his veins that made him regardless of all external influences.

As he held Isolt with linked fingers, had the pressure he had given been answered ? As the lightning flashed out of his eyes, had there been a corresponding flash in hers ? As his heart bounded, had her pulses beat in rhythm to his ?

What was this sensation which had come on him ? A rush of fire had enveloped him, dazzled his eyes, maddened his brain, made his heart drunk. What was it all ?—love ? Or was he intoxicated, electrified by the look, the touch, of this girl, Isolt ? It was told of the old miners that they had taken hemp-seed, had strewn it on live coals, and had inhaled the fumes that rose from the burning grains, and had gone raging mad. He had heard of a man who had looked into the lightning, and had been ever after beside himself. Had her breath the intoxicating power of hemp-seed, her glance the maddening effect of the lightning ?

The wolf trotted at his side, and looked inquiringly at his master. He snuffed, then turned, and rubbed his snout against the boots of Guavas. The miner heeded him not.

The rushes and rank grass in swampy places, hard frozen, crackled under his tread. The moss, usually spongy, now full of ice particles, was crunched beneath his feet.

A night heron rose, and on broad wings rushed away. The wolf dashed after it, but found that the bird was beyond reach and returned to his master's side.

Suddenly, roused from his dream, he knew not by what, Eldad looked around him and became aware that he was on a wrong track. He had walked forward, as he believed in the right direction, but it is not easy on rolling moor, where are no landmarks distinguishable by night, to observe a proper course. He had gone out of his way and where he was he did not know. A river was brawling below him in a valley, but what river this was he could not decide. If he had gone due south after crossing the Western Dart, which he had done, then he should not have come on another stream flowing athwart his course.

How long had he been walking ? An hour ? half an hour ? Eldad had been so engrossed in his thoughts that he had lost all count of time. He did not know where he had diverged from the right track—a track indeed only discernible by day, and then only at intervals.

Whereabouts was he ? How was he to recover his direction ? Guavas looked up at the sky. A film of white cloud had formed over it, and though it did not extinguish the moon, it obscured its light, and made the discovery of its direction difficult to the strayed man. Perplexed, angry with himself, the miner faced round to the wind. That had blown from the north when he started in the afternoon to walk over the frosted moor to Crockern Hall. He had not observed whether it came from the same point as he left; it was possible that the wind might have shifted in the little space of time since he began his return journey.

Another element of uncertainty connected with the wind lay in this, that it gave but one line of direction and, supposing it remained constant, it would indicate the course to south which Guavas must pursue, but it gave no clue as to how far he had swerved to east or to west, before he discovered that he was at fault.

Eldad seated himself on a block of granite. The hill-side descended rapidly to the stream below. He could not see the water, only a congeries of blots and blotches that represented masses of stone, over and through and under which the water worked its way.

When, on waste land, one has completely lost bearings a sense of giddiness and a sinking of the heart ensue. The world does not seem turned upside down, but spun round so that all sense as to whither the course should be directed is gone. In such cases the rule given on the moors is to follow the water.

But to follow a vagrant stream that would indeed lead to inhabited land, but which might lead to land twenty miles distant from the point sought, such an alternative is only to be adopted in desperation. Perhaps when enveloped in fog, hardly when the outline of hill and tor is distinguishable.

Guavas passed his hand across his face, to brush

away the cobweb of dreams that had bewildered him. He was a man of resolution, and he put from him the thought of Isolt, and fixed his attention on present circumstances.

He looked on all sides, in endeavour to recognise some natural feature, but though the profile of the moors was distinctly pencilled against the grey sky, yet there was absolutely no conspicuous object, no rock, no cairn that could give him an idea as to where he was and whence he had swerved from his right course.

No sound was audible save the rush of the river, and the occasional cry of a plover, with the moan of the wind among the frosted grass.

As Guavas saw no feature of the country that could give him his course, he was constrained to obey the common injunction in such cases and follow the stream ; but he was well resolved to follow it no further than to the first habitation.

Accordingly he kept along the height above the stream, dipping into an occasional lateral combe, and then reascending the hill opposite till, finally, he caught a glimpse of a light.

He quickened his steps and descended the slope, then reached a wall of unhewn granite stones piled one on another enclosing a piece of reclaimed land ; thereupon he was suddenly assailed by furious barks, and in another moment a large dog was on the wall with bristling hairs, threatening attack, uncertain which to assail first —the man or the wolf.

At once a door was opened, and a woman's voice was heard calling : " Who comes at night ? Be still, Guy."

The dog was ill disposed to obey, but reiterated commands forced him to leap down and go to his mistress's side in the house door.

When Eldad Guavas came to the door, and looked in, a strange sight met his eyes—a scene of death.

In the chamber lay a corpse, with the feet towards the door, and two candles at the head and one at the feet. It lay in a board coffin, with a plate of salt and a loaf on the breast. Many old women were in the apartment, wailing, singing, declaiming, and the hubbub was only arrested by the appearance of the miner, with 'his wolf, in the doorway.

"Come in !" said the woman who had restrained her dog. " But first tie up that creature of thine or he and mine will fight, and that ill beseems a house of mourning. My good man is dead, and will be carried forth on the morrow."

Eldad hesitated.

"I need," he said, "but direction ; give me that and I will go on."

"Nay," answered the woman, "that were to bring ill luck to the house, and no rest to my man, not to enter and eat of the soul-cake, and drink a draught of aqua vitæ. God hath brought thee hither, and here thou must tarry awhile."

Eldad consented. On such an occasion it would have caused offence not to partake of the general meal. He chained up the wolf in an out-house and entered the room.

This was small, close, and crowded.

An old woman stood up, and, bending over the coffin said in the ear of the corpse : "They have made thee a rare good chamber out to Widicombe Churchyard, and no thought o' cost in it. I reckon thou'lt be rarely comfortable there, and as volks goeth by o' Sundays, they'll say, 'Deary life ! who lieth there ? What ! old Captain Ford ! He's well and vittily laid sure enough, and above his station. I reckon any man would be proud o' such a bed as he's gotten, and take good care he will not quit it lest some other ghost clip in and occupy it while he be wandering else-where."

Then up stood another old woman, and ex-claimed : "You needn't trouble and worrit about the widow and the orphan, Captain Ford. There's a cow and a pig and half a score o' ewes, and they'll be very comfortable, and none occasion at all for you to fret yourself and come back out o' glory, and see after they. Thanks be that you have provided for them. I reckon they'll manage bravely for themselves, and you lie aisy and don't fash your head about the consarns o' this mortal life no more. I'm sure you're goin' to a better place, where there'll be figgy puddin' better than ever was biled in this here vale o' tears."

"And what a thing it be to be buried respectable!" exclaimed a third, "and nothin' spared to make all pleasant all round. A little drop o' aqua vitæ to drink a suant voyage to the departed, and that he may enjoy hisself just as us does here! and no figs spared in his soul-cake, and spice and ginger, my dear blood! I'd be proud to die if I wor to be buried and gie' so much pleasure all round at my buryin'."

"An' what a gude man he wor—the Cap'n; so gude to the poor," said another. "I mind when her (he) gi'ed me as much rishes (rushes) cut by hisself as iver I wanted for my datchin, and he wor that charitable when her killed a sheep, her sent me the pluck. May he be received into glory—and bide there."

"And," threw in the first, "well he may be given to glory, when everything as he cu'd wish for in heaven and airth is provided reg'lar. Here be a strange man come in as'll take all his sins away as might ha' made a bit o' a difficulty wi' the porter to Heaven's gates. Will ye now just stand there?" she asked, signing to Guavas.

The miner, unwilling to object to anything that might be asked of him, answered : "I will do what is required, but I demand first that I may be directed on my way to Yealm Steps. I have a long stretch of moor to make this night."

"Well," said the same woman in reply, "us'll take care for that. For sure certain the little maid can guide'y to Childe's Cross, and from there you can get along o' your self. But first you must eat the soul-cake, and so tak' the dead man's sins on ye. 'Taint a terrible lot—he were a main gude man."

The woman took up a broad saffron cake that lay on the dead man's breast, broke it, and passed it across the coffin to Guavas.

He received the portion and ate some mouthfuls, whilst all the company looked on in silence. Then the same woman passed to him a bowl of spirits across the coffin, and Guavas gratefully drank it. When he had done, all present raised a cry, and threw at him sticks, cinders, whatever they could lay hold of, and he was hustled on all sides and thrust out of the door.

"He has taken on him the sins o' the dead!
Cast'n out!" was the general cry.[1]

[1] The custom of "sin-eating" was still practised in Aubrey's
time in Herefordshire and Shropshire, and was only then expir-
ing in Wales where it had been universal. The "Soul-cakes"
remained in use elsewhere, after their significance had been lost.
There is no direct evidence that "sin-eating" was practised
in Devon, but certain indications point in that direction, and as
the race occupying Cornwall and a part of Devon was identical with
that in Wales, it is probable that this singular custom was at one
time common there likewise. I have ventured to suppose that it
was lingering on at the period of the reign of Queen Elizabeth,
in such a remote and isolated region as Dartmoor. For an account of the custom, see Aubrey, "Remains of Gentilisme and
Judaisme" (Folk Lore Society, 1881); also Leland's "Collectanea,"
quoted by Brand, "Popular Antiquities," ii. 246, Bohn's Edition.

CHAPTER VII

LEMONDAY

ELDAD stood outside the door, astonished and angry. The custom of "sin-eating" was not one about which Guavas understood anything. It was pursued here and there only, where old women were allowed to have the management of the death-chamber and the conduct of a funeral, in those portions of the land most removed from civilisation and where old pagan practices lingered unaltered by Catholicism or undissolved by Protestantism. On Dartmoor, a vast tract of moorland nominally in the parish of Lydford many miles distant, where the church was accessible by one track only carried betwixt unsoundable bogs, the natives had lived for centuries entirely untouched by religious influences, following traditional usages that dated back to the first occupation of Britain by the rude stone monument builders and handed on by them to their Celtic conquerors.

To eat of the funeral feast was a duty. To refuse it was to proclaim a feud that was deadly and unpardonable. Guavas had readily complied with the request or demand of the woman who acted as stewardess of the ceremonies to partake of the soul-cake, but he was unprepared to accept the consequences and be regarded and treated as a sort of scapegoat taking on him the sins of the deceased.

He was not a superstitious man; nevertheless, there was something disquieting in the thought that he had unwittingly incurred responsibilities he had not desired, or at all events had taken a prominent part in a rite that had no sanction in Christianity, Catholic or Reformed, and which savoured of something much opposed to its principles.

He stood outside the door, doubtful what to do, when it opened and a girl came forth. She was aged about eighteen, had fair hair with a golden tinge in it that shone as the light glinted on it from within, and with a beautifully formed oval face.

"I am going to show thee the way to Childe's Cross," said the girl. "I am Lemonday, and they do not wish to have me within; I cry too much for dear father, and they frighten me with their strange ways."

"You are sent to direct me?"

"Yes—you have lost your course."

It was characteristic of the time and of the discipline maintained on the moor, that the thought of peril to the young girl, going alone at night over the waste with a strange man, occurred to none, not even to her mother. No instance was known at that time of a wrong done by a miner to an innocent and harmless maiden. Every man knew that such a transgression would be visited by the whole body in a terrible manner. A tradition remained of such a vengeance, when the transgressor was surrounded in his hut and burnt alive, faggots of furze having been heaped about the walls and thrown over the roof and set fire to. When this had occurred—whether during the Wars of the Roses, or even earlier—was not known. In oral tradition historic perspective does not exist.

"I am come to show the way," said the girl. "We must e'en cross the river."

"What river is this that brawls below? and where are we now?" asked Eldad.

"The river is but a small one," answered the girl, "and for a name they call it the Strane, and this, my mother's house, and where my father dwelled, is Swancombe."

Then Guavas was aware how greatly he had diverged from the direct course; he had worked to the left considerably and had struck on an affluent of the Dart, already a stream of. some volume, whereas he should have directed his way across the moor in which the river Strane rises.

"In Heaven's name! I am out," said he.

"Whence comest thou?"

"From Tinners' Hall."

"Then, indeed, thou art astray if thou wouldst to Yealm Head and so down to the Steps. What is that noise?"

The wolf was howling.

"It is even my companion and child," answered Guavas. "That is my tame wolf, and I trow it is the very last of the kind in all England. There had been one on the Cornish Moors—by Kilmar; it was a dam; the mate had already been killed— but come! I will tell thee this as we walk along. I must unbridle Loup."

"Will he not do me a hurt?"

"He is under control. I will hold him by the chain if thou fearest."

"I do indeed fear. I prithee hold him chained."

Accordingly Guavas unbound the wolf from the rack to which it had been attached, and, gathering up the light chain in his hand, bade the brute walk at his side. Thereupon the girl frankly took her place on the other side.

"My dear father is dead," she said, "and to-morrow they will carry him to Widicombe." [1] She sobbed, "he was a good father to me."

"And there is no loss to a maid greater than that of a father, save only that of a mother."

"I thank God she is still in good health," said the girl.

"And now shall I tell thee more of my wolf ?"

"If it pleaseth you. But first must we cross the river. Give me your hand, for here is the ford."

"Nay, I want no help from a little maid. I can cross by myself unassisted. And the water is but shallow."

"There are stone steps," said Lemonday, "and, see, the moon is breaking out, and thou canst see them."

"That is well—and I can see something better."

"What is that ?"

"Thy innocent and sweet face."

Lemonday cast down her eyes, sorely abashed.

[1] Although the entire moor is in the parish of Lydford, owing to the impracticability of conveying corpses to the churchyard there except in favourable weather, by grant of Bishop Brones-combe in 1260 the dead were allowed to be buried at Widicombe instead.

She was unaccustomed to compliments; they distressed her.

"Thou wast about to tell me of the wolf," she said.

"It is well; we will speak of the wolf when we have crossed the water. Let me help thee over."

"Nay!" laughed Lemonday. "I am a maid of the moor, and such be able to manage without assistance in a matter so light as this."

She leaped with unerring exactness from one stone to another, where a slip and a fall might have entailed bruises if not have broken bones. She was like a bird skipping—like a wagtail—and so light was her step, so easy her swing, that it seemed as though she flew. Guavas was constrained to follow with more caution and slowly.

On reaching the further side, Lemonday began to climb the steep ascent. "Now," said she, "tell me concerning the wolf."

"That," answered Guavas, "must again be deferred. This climb takes all my breath, and I have none to spare for speech, but thou—if thou art light in mind as in foot—art a very wanton."

"I have no lightness in my heart, God wot!" she said. "My dear father, the best of men, is dead, and if I had lightness before, it be all quenched out of me now. Nay—at times the tears so swell up in my heart that I must sit down and weep my eyes out. Then I sing, Well-a-day! to fight against my sorrow. Alack! How shall my mother and I live without him?"

"Nay, doubt not," answered Guavas. "To thy mother the death of her husband is the putting out of her light, but not to thee. Thou art young, and to the young comes hope, and, better than that, Love will fly as surely as the butterfly cometh to the flower. I shall live yet to see his golden wings flutter above thy pretty crown."

She shook her head.

"Aye—shake thy head, but the time will come. To every young maid it comes as surely as to the old comes death."

"What—and not to the man?"

"Let the men be—we talk now of maids."

"Nay, verily, if that wanton Love comes to us maids, I doubt not he beats his wings at your windows also."

"That may be. I have never seen the glint of his glittering wings yet at Yealm Steps."

"Nor I neither in Swancombe Bottom."

"Who knows? he may come some day when you least reckon, and from a quarter whence you least look for him."

The girl shrugged her shoulders.

"May the day be distant. I live with my mother, and must comfort her now that father is gone. But that I have lost a father, I would say I am happy—I want nothing more."

"Not even a lover?"

"Nay, I can do without and be thankful. With love comes sorrow they say; and I had no sorrow till father fell ill. But think of that! Thou mayst well chide me for lightness; my dear father lies dead, and I speak of such fond things as love."

"It was I who spake thereon. But alack! I can no more, I can speak no more climbing this hill."

But even this maid was at last out of breath; she had picked up the skirt of her gown and looped it under the girdle about her waist, lest she should trip on the sharp ascent.

As she was silent, her thoughts recurred to the death-chamber, to the dead man lying there, and to the wailing of the mourners, and her sobs broke out afresh.

The man she conducted heard her sobs, and sought occasion to divert her thoughts into another channel.

They had reached a more gentle ascent, and Eldad was able to proceed with his tale.

"There is not much to relate," said he. "The

wolf comes from the Cornish moors under Kilmar. The old father was killed there in the marshes; but the dam remained unslain, and I and others there set to hunt for her, and we found that she had made a layer under one of the old men's graves that they call Shilstones. We slew the wolf, and she had young with her. All these we killed save one, which I kept, and, as there is verily no other wolf in all Devon or Cornwall, it matters not, for the breed will die with Loup."

"Who is Loup?"

"That is my wolf. I so name him. I was told by the clerk that it was a French or Latin name, and meant the same as wolf in English."

"And you brought up the beast from a cub?"

"Yes; it has ever been with me; it has fed from my hand, and when I sleep lies at my feet."

"Yet you chain him."

"I chain him lest he fall on and harm others. He has a tooth for a lamb or a sheep, and may get me much ill-will and cost me money. I cannot break him of what was planted in his nature. Therefore, I am obliged to keep him under restraint."

Thus they continued talking as they pursued their way.

And now the moon had unveiled herself, and looked down out of a clear sky, in which twinkled a few stars set far apart.   As already said, the moon was in crescent, but a crescent that was filling her horns, and she threw down sufficient light to make the snow patches gleam like her own face.

The moor was broad, undulating, unstrewn with granite, and seemed to stretch away into infinite space.   It had on it no apparent way marks.

"Dost thou know the ballet of Childe the Hunter?" asked Lemonday, "for shortly we shall be at his grave."

"I have heard the tale," answered Guavas, "but would fain hear it again from thy lips."

"Nay, I should spoil the tale, for doubtless thou hast heard it better told than I can frame it, and to sing the ballad I list not, for here we are, and it would hold us too long in the sharp wind."

She halted at a mass of rocks arranged by art to form a rude chamber or coffin.

"Here," she said, "we must part.   Yonder is thy way—thou canst hardly go wrong; but bear not to the right or thou runnest into Foxtor Mire."

"Stay," said Guavas.   "Turn thy sweet face to the moon that I may well see to whom I owe the favour and the kindness of guidance."

He took the maiden by the shoulder, dropping the chain and putting his foot on it, and he turned Lemonday about that he might observe her.

The face was wondrous comely, and beautifully shaped.

Eldad looked steadily at it, and would have looked longer had the girl not shaken herself free.

"I'feck!" she said, "I think thou hast looked thy fill."

"I could look till the moon went down, and then curse her for setting," said Guavas; "and now for a Cornishman's salutation as we part. Dost' know what that is?"

"Something wondrous civil, as I take it, if thou be a Cornishman."

"The salutation of a Cornishman to his enemy is—a blow."

"But to a friend?"

"To one he loves—a kiss on the red lips."

"I'faith—I will neither one nor the other."

"But to one whom he reverences"—he stopped and raised his hands to his lips. "*This* to the Priest, the King, and to the White Maid."

CHAPTER VIII

GOLD-DUST

STRANGE it was that during the first portion of his walk that night the mind of Guavas had been filled with one woman, and that during the second portion of his walk he thought only of another. The thought of Isolt had caused him to stray, and Lemonday had conducted him into his right course. He was at first like one who had drunk fire that ran through all his veins in flame; he was now as one soothed by a fresh breeze blowing over a bank of wild thyme.

The converse of the two maidens was as unlike as might well be. Isolt had spoken mainly of the finding of gold and tin in the pitch at Yealm Steps, and, however much Eldad might seek to change the subject, she ever reverted thereto; so that a man less interested than Guavas might well have thought that she concerned herself with him more because he was accounted a prosperous

miner than for any merit she discovered in himself.

But with Lemonday no word had been spoken
concerning mining prospects ; her thoughts were
entirely free from desire to ascertain whether the
man she was guiding were fortunate in his ventures or unhappy. Her manner, her tone of
voice, her matter of speech were all fresh, simple,
and childlike. Converse with Isolt had made
Eldad giddy, but that with Lemonday had cleared
his mind.

He strode along his way with confidence. He
was no longer liable to go astray.

If he had not thus come on and been associated
for a little while with Lemonday, he would have
still had his head and heart enveloped in the
vapours conjured up by that enchantress Isolt.
He had indeed been in a magic world ; but the
voice, the touch of Lemonday had recovered him.

He arrived safely at his house—if house the
hovel could be called in which à tinner was content to dwell whilst on his pitch. He moved
from place to place as his claim proved profitable
or not. Therefore, he felt no necessity to do more
than throw up four walls and roof them over.
The roof was itself of poles and rushes, to be
renewed each year, for every year it was committed to the flames to recover out of it the

particles of tin that had been carried up with the smoke of the furnace and had been deposited in the thatch.

A thatch thus burnt yielded on an average ten pounds' worth of tin, so great was the waste under the old system of smelting.

Eldad found his mother awaiting him, and anxious to hear whether he had amused himself and had chosen some wench who might take her place when she failed.

" Mother," said Eldad, in reply to her close questioning, " Verily I have seen two damsels, and each is so comely and each so engaging, yet each so different from other, that, as Heaven is above me, I know not to which I can lay my fancy; and therefore, good mother, I shall be wise to keep away from one and the other lest perhaps, if fastened to one, I should wish myself attached to the other."

During the early spring the old woman's health rapidly declined, and she died at Easter.

Eldad had been dearly linked to his mother; he had been a tender and devoted son, and she died blessing him. The last breath left her with her hand on his bowed head.

After this he was alone, and was constrained to cook his own food and clean his own cabin, in addition to his work in the stream bed.

Care for his mother, as well as pressure of work, had detained Eldad at Yealm Steps, and he made no attempt to see again either of the women who had in one night exercised such strange and contrary influences on him. Although he was alone owner of his claim, or "pitch," as is the West country term for a plot of ground worked for metal, yet Eldad had workmen termed "spalliers" under him, to whom he paid a wage. These men lived or lodged in the farmhouses that bordered on the moor, and came to their work by daybreak from a little distance and returned at sundown. As the common or down where Guavas and Rawle had their pitches was not on the forest of Dartmoor, but on the common of Cornwood, the distance was by no means so considerable for the men to journey to their work as in other cases.

The vast tract of Dartmoor actually consists of the forest, so called because it was a wilderness roamed over at one time by deer, and the commons of Devon that engirdle it, the united area of which is quite as extensive as the forest itself.

The forest belongs to the Duchy of Cornwall, and is owned by the Prince of Wales as Duke of Cornwall, and when there is no Prince of Wales then held by the Crown. The Duchy claims an overlordship over all the commons, which overlordship has been from time immemorial disputed by the lords of the manors of the several parishes adjoining the forest that include these commons, as well as by the commoners themselves—that is to say, by the parishioners, who assert over these commons immemorial rights of free pasturage and turbary, or the right to obtain thence fuel for their hearths ; also the right to carry off what granite lies on the surface for building purposes, but not to quarry.

Conflicts of rights has resulted from time to time in conflicts of force. When the Duchy sends its servants to "drive" the commons—that is, to sweep together the cattle found on them and to impound them—the farmers of the parishes and the servants of the lord of the manor assemble and resist the officers of the Duchy. Such fights have occurred recently, and sometimes one side obtains the mastery, sometimes the other. Neither side proceeds against the other by law, because neither has any documentary evidence to establish its rights.

Eldad was not only the sole holder of a " pitch " and employer of labour, digging out stream tin and crushing and washing it, but he also smelted his own metal.

This was not always done. In every valley of a stream that flows from Dartmoòr were at least two, usually more, " blowing-houses." These were often owned by a company of streamers, who employed a blower to smelt the ore from their several claims, which ore was sent to the blowing-house in bags attached to the necks of dogs. The blower knew whose consignment of "black tin" he received because he knew each dog and to whom it belonged.

Now it was remarked that Guavas was not content to send his tin to be smelted at the blowing-house, which lay but a bowshot off above the cataract, but erected one for himself in which he might reduce his own metal. This, in itself, roused suspicion. Why should he have his own blowing-house when another was close at hand, unless he desired to conceal what he found, and keep from the knowledge of others the greatness and richness of his find ?

His spalliers were disposed to brag, and their idle boasts encouraged and deepened the belief that Guavas had lighted on a deposit of extraordinary value.

It was the duty of the bailiff to make a circuit of the works of the several miners at intervals, and to look at their accumulations of tin and their method of working. If the mine or the streaming were conducted properly and not wastefully he cut a notch on the windlass of the mine, or the wooden post erected by the claim of the

away, then he desisted altogether from making such propositions.

"It is well," said he;" "let each stand on his own feet and not sit astride on the shoulders of another !"

One day, to his great surprise, as Guavas looked up from the trench in the rubble, where he was working, he saw Isolt Rodda seated on a black moor pony, on the top of a heap of refuse, looking down on him. With riding in the wind her hair had become disengaged and flowed down her back and was waved around her by the wind. She was extraordinarily handsome, and at once an electric shock ran through the Cornishman's frame. He dropped his "physgie" (pick) and mounted the heap of rubble, removed his pointed, fur-bound cap, and stood before her, speechless.

"Master Guavas !" said she, smiling encouragingly. "As thou hast never come to see me since that evening in midwinter, I have come to visit thee, and to see the gold thou didst tell me of."

"The gold !" repeated Eldad. "Surely, Mistress Isolt, I made no brag of gold. This is a tin floor."

"Aye ! and thou findest no gold ? Didst thou not show me thy gold ring ? See, thou hast it now on thy finger. That was made from the finds here. I have come to ask thee to show me the gold in grain, or ever it be cast into a ring. In troth, I reckon that there is little gold elsewhere. Some do say that in the haunted mine of the Romans in Chaw Gulley, where the ravens nest, that there is much gold, but a devil keeps guard lest any touch it, and a dragon sits thereon and hatches out ever and ever more gold."

"Gold !" repeated Eldad, with a laugh. "It is but little gold I find here."

"Nay—but surely thou hast some to show me ? I have never cast eyes on the grain."

" I will show you what I have. It is but a little dust of gold, a very little."

" How much hast thou ?"

"Nay—thou wilt laugh to hear how little."

" I will laugh to think how sly thou art."

" I protest ; I have but one quill-ful."

" I protest ; thou hast a score in hiding. Nay, it matters not. Thou wilt not tell, even to me. Show me the little that thou hast. I am fain to see it."

Guavas went to his hut, and presently emerged with a goose-quill that was charged with the golden particles and was sealed with wax.

"This," he said, "will I gladly give thee in remembrance of the converse I had with thee, and because I held thee back when thou wouldst dance."

"Nay, in God's name," said Isolt, "I will not take it; there is too much to be wasted, and too little to fashion into a ring."

She looked steadily into his eyes; he could not endure their light, and his fell on the goose-quill he held.

"It is true," said he, "there is not enough for a ring."

"And so this is all?" she asked, and kept her eyes fixed on him.

He said nothing. He was afraid to look at her again. He thought of the little maid at Swancombe. That kept his lips sealed. They were sealed so long as he avoided looking into that beautiful, that spell-working face.

She turned her horse with a mocking laugh.

"You Cornishmen!" she scoffed, "I had heard tell ye were all gallants. It is a lie; ye are false and grasping, and sorry knaves."

When he looked up she was away. Then he thought that he had not behaved towards the Bargmaster's daughter with the graciousness that was seemly.

"I will make amends," said he. "I am a poor awkward fool! I will give her a May-bush. She will pardon me."

CHAPTER IX

"ON A MAY MORNING SO EARLY"

IT was the custom in England on May morning
early for youths to go before the windows of
the maids they admired, and there to carol and
plant a bush that was in flower. When the damsel
favoured a suit she would come forth and offer
the swain a bowl of curds and cream.

The practice somewhat extended itself beyond
its original purport; not only real suitors for a
maid's favour, but all such as desired to show
respect and pay homage to a maiden, without
ulterior object, would contribute their flowering
boughs; and a girl was proud who could say that
many waved under her window, and that many
voices united in carolling her beauty and amia-
bility.

Moreover, that maiden thought herself ill used
who received no such recognition of her merits.

Those who had contributed their green bushes

might calculate on a dance round the Maypole the same afternoon with the maid they had honoured; and just as certainly was he refused who had not thought it worth his while to offer his homage on May morning at the rising of the sun.

Eldad Guavas had never hitherto taken any share in such performances. He had not frequented the Maypole, and he had never cared for any girl sufficiently to trouble himself to rise early and decorate her door with the May-bush.

But now it was otherwise. He felt that something was due to Isolt, the daughter of the bailiff, not only because she was the bailiff's daughter, but because she had singled him out for her gracious regard, she had honoured him above her recognised suitors at the Tinner's Hall, and she had visited him at his works.

He had been down into Cornwood the day before, and had begged some spring flowers, and with these he decorated a bough that was covered with fresh leaves; and very early before the break of day he made his way to the house of the Bargmaster with a heart fluttering with emotion.

The spell of that beautiful woman was still on him, and repeatedly did her face shine out upon him in the dark or start to recognition from among the granite heaps.

What was he that he should dream of such a

girl ! He a poor Cornish miner, whereas she was the daughter of an official in great power under the Duchy ; one lived from hand to mouth, dependent on chance, the other in an assured and tolerably lucrative position. One alone and helpless among envious strangers, the other child of a man supreme in his control of all the miners—or supreme, in fact, if not by right. Nominally under the control of the Warden of the Stannaries, Rodda was actually left to the unchecked exercise of his own will.

And Isolt was unquestionably the most splendid woman he had ever seen, with a force in her that carried all before her, against which he felt himself powerless. Did he love her ? He dared not ask himself the question. At the thought of her his head reeled, his pulse bounded. He feared her because he knew that he could never win her— that she could but plunge him in hopeless misery.

As he approached her house, he saw others there —Dickon Rawle, Humphrey Evea, and two whom he did not recognise in the white raw light of morning. His heart contracted with pain. He had foolishly hoped to forestall all others, and win for himself alone that recognition she seemed so willing to accord him. But though he craved for this, he feared it, lest it should still further fire his blood and madden his brain.

"Thou art here, Cornish chough?" mocked Evea. "What is thy croak like? We are warblers, and you of the crow nature. Canst sing a part in a Threeman's song? If so, Dickon and you and I will sing together."

"What will the song be?"

"The song of May."

"It is well. I can take my part."

Then the three, holding their boughs set with flowers and ribbons, sang together a carol that may still be heard in the west :—

> Awake, my pretty maid, awake,
>   Refreshed from drowsy dream,
> And haste to dairy house, and take
>   For us a dish of cream.
> If not a dish of yellow cream,
>   Then give us kisses three,
> The woodland bower is white with flower,
>   And green is every tree.
>
> Awake, awake, my pretty maid,
>   And take the May-bush in,
> Or 'twill be gone ere to-morrow morn,
>   And you'll have none within.
> Throughout the night, before the light,
>   There fell the dew or rain,
> It trembles bright, on May-bush white
>   It sparkles on the plain.

The house door opened, and Isolt came fortn attended by a maid. She bore in her hands a bowl of cream, and her servant a platter heaped with cakes.

"I thank you, good sirs," she said and smiled, addressing Eldad. "And I pray you refresh yourselves after your labours."

She handed the bowl to Guavas and accepted his bough. Then turning to the maid said, "Attend on their necessities, I must return within"; and she retired carrying the branch of Guavas in her hand.

The Cornishman was drinking the cream, and did not see the angry glances exchanged by his rivals. When he had quenched his thirst, and passed the bowl to his fellow tinner, the bailiff's daughter was no longer there, and his bough was gone.

The favour shown him surprised and confused him. He was aware that this would provoke at least banter, probably a quarrel with the two men along with whom he had sung in part the May carol; and to avoid either alternative, each equally distasteful, he at once walked away in another direction from that along which he knew they would return.

May Day was a holiday, when no work was done, and he had therefore no particular desire to return to his own habitation.

He, therefore, struck over the moors to the north without at first having any definite notion whither he would betake himself, but presently he thought of Lemonday in Swancombe, and he fell a-wondering how many youths had sung carols under her window and had offered her their May-boughs.

Moved partly by a wish to ascertain this, partly also by a desire to revisit the house of mourning, when he himself was in bereavement, as a place more congenial to him than the riotous gatherings of merry-makers, for which he had no lust, he quickened his steps. After a look about him to determine his direction he ascended the long ridge in the morasses, at the head of which all those streams rise which run directly south into the sea without any bends to east and to north. Such are the Avon, the Erme, and the Yealm.

The elevation of the moor, its exposure, made it very barren both of vegetation and of flower at this early time of the year ; only the golden furze was in bloom, and the little milkwort was expanding its changeful flowers, pink and blue and white. The silver cotton grass, where the white heads remained, was draggled with the winter rains, and had lost its beauty and gloss, and hung like little tufts of wet wool. The heather, leafless and brown, seemed dead past recovering to life ; the very grass was sere and had not begun to bud. The milkwort was sparse, but yet it flowered, and was welcome because no other flower was to be seen save the never-failing furze.

The stray spots of colour attracted Eldad's eye, and he stooped at intervals and picked the tiny flower. Time was now no object to him, so he got a rush, and with a fine thread he bound the little flowers to the rush, and wondrously varied in tone they were—no two of the same tint.

He halted, engaged with his little posy, and as he made it up he whistled the May carol. The larks were singing overhead.

The sun had risen, and the sky was clear. All promised a perfectly beautiful May Day. The warm rays striking on him were grateful. Every rush and grass blade and stem of heather was strung with drops that twinkled with as many colours as there were in the milkwort blossoms.

Presently he reached the tomb of Childe the Hunter, and now he became impatient to be at his destination. He had tarried too long. All the carollers would be gone. He would be too late to see whom little Lemonday favoured.

The slope of the moor was now towards the north, and what water there was in pools and marshes inclined to flow in an opposite direction to that in which it had run in the earlier portion of the tinner's walk. Then he came to a steeper decline and saw Swanscombe open before him, and below, near the river, nestling under a shoulder of rock-strewn hill, the cottage or farmstead of the Fords.

And now Guavas stood still and listened, but heard no strain of song. He was too late. The carollers had departed. He shaded his eyes to look. He could discern no bough beside the door. But what of that? Lemonday had taken in that of the swain she approved. He almost ran down the slope, and he leaped from rock to rock in the bed of the stream, and breathless stood before the door and saw before him the fair form of the girl, slender, fresh-complexioned, neat in dress, and without a straying hair—sweet, pure, beautiful as one of the milkworts he held in his posy.

"So—I am come again, Lemonday," said he, flushing with pleasure.

"And who are you?" she answered, but smiled knowingly as she spake, showing her white teeth, and her blue eyes twinkled.

"It is I—Guavas, the tinner. Dost thou not recall me, Lemonday?"

She replied, "Consider, thou hast the advantage. At Childe's Tomb thou didst turn me about to face the moon; but, as for thee, I could not take thy shoulders and twist thee that I might look at the fashion of thy face. I knew thee not, verily, as thou camest before my eyes, but by the tone of thy voice I knew thee at once. Thou art welcome with all my heart."

She extended to him both her hands. He took both, still holding the little posy of milkwort tied to a rush ; and when he released her, he left the flowers in her hand.

She looked at the little bunch. "It is rarely assorted," she said. "Is that for me ?"

"Aye, maid !" he answered, "Is not this May Day ?"

Then he sang a snatch of the carol.

> "Awake, awake, fair, pretty maid,
> And take the May-bush in,
> Or 'twill be gone ere to-morrow morn,
> And you'll have none within."

"But there now, pretty maid," he said, "I come over late and bring thee but a simple posy ; whereas others have been before me and have given thee gay-decked boughs. How many have been here ?"

She laughed and said, "None—none ever come here."

"What—and thou hast no May posy ?"

"Nay, I have a very choice one—it is this."

He gave a shout of joy—why he did not know —and she said hastily—lest he, in his joy, should give her such a Cornish salute as she cared not to receive—" I must even go to the dairy and bring thee curds and cream."

"Then," said he, "let us eat them together on this bench in the bright morning sun."

CHAPTER X

THE KEENLY LODE

WHEN Lemonday came forth with bread and milk into the brilliant sunshine, Guavas was already seated on the little bench.

He smiled and signed to her, and she seated herself beside him, holding the milk bowl on her lap. She had stuck the bunch of milkwort in her bosom.

"My mother is from home," she said; "she went away before dawn to Widicombe."

"What, on May morning, and leave thee alone when all the lads are fluttering around the fair maids."

"Ah, fie! none such come this way. That mother knoweth right well. This is such a wisht (lonesome) lost place that none care to seek it out, leastways to find naught better than such as me. But I take it kindly that thou hast thought of us and come hither. And, indeed, we owe thee a duty, for thou didst eat my father's sins. God help him ! he was a good man and never did harm to any. So thou hast had no heavy burden to bear, if thou didst carry them away."

" Lemonday, that is a fond and foolish custom, if it be not a curst one. There is but One who can take away sin, and that is not a poor erring man such as I."

" I trow you speak right," said the girl, gravely. " But it is an old usage."

" Our forefathers did this because they knew no better and lived in superstition and the shadow of ignorance."

" That may be ; nay, for very surety it is so. But I prithee eat a curd and drink."

" I drink to thee in the innocent sweet milk," he said.

She saw that he partook with pleasure. She smiled, and said, " Hast thou had nothing between thy lips this morn ? "

He coloured and hesitated. But he was a truthful and honest man, and he would conceal nothing. Therefore, he replied : " I have already had a bowl and broken bread. I went a-Maying to the house of the bailiff's daughter."

" Ah ! " she said, without any token of disappointment or jealous twinge, " I hear she is the Queen of the Forest. I have never seen her. Tell me what she is like."

"I have not come hither to speak of her," answered Guavas somewhat impatiently.

Then the girl was silent.

Presently she said, as the silence became irksome, "And so thou art a tinner. I knew not that."

"Yes ; I am a tinner at Yealm Steps."

"That thou camest from Yealm Steps I conjectured, as that is the place to which I directed thee the night afore my dear father was buried. He was once a tinner also. I am glad I helped thee for his sake. One tinner stands by another."

"One and all," answered Guavas ; "yet they only hold together and help one another when they belong to the same parts. I am a Cornishman, and I have met with little regard and no friendship here. Instead of help I get contradiction."

"If my father had lived, he would have stood by thee. But in the end he was no more a tinner. They called him a captain, but he had nothing to do with mines for many years."

"Why did he give up mining ? "

"Because of my mother. When he married her she had this little tenement, but she was very poor, and he, with the savings of the tin he had found, was able to buy a few sheep and a cow and to stock it. So he settled down to attend to the farm, and went no more to ball."[1]

"Where was the ball (mine) in which he worked ?"

"It is at some distance hence. I cannot say for sure. It is east, away by Hameldon, I think; but I have never been there."

"Was he with many adventurers ?"

"He was alone."

"Alone ! and a mine ? That is not possible."

"It is truth. It was an old ball. I will tell about it. My father did stream-work once, and he found out a way of catching the tin out of the smoke instead of burning the roof every year."

"How was that ?" inquired Eldad eagerly.

"He made a kind of chimney in a bank that turned about. He had a book, and he drew a picture therein to show his plan. Then all the sparkles of tin, instead of going into the roof, settled in places, elbows of the chimney, and were brushed out."

"This is wonderful !" exclaimed Guavas, with flashing eyes. "Your father was a shrewd man."

"He discovered other things. Thou knowest men like not to be put out of their old ways. So was it with such as worked with father. They kept from him and laughed and flouted at him

---

[1] "To ball "=to mine.

for what he discovered. Thou knowest how hard the charges fall on the miners. They be lightened somewhat now, but under King Henry the miners were trodden down in every way. They had hard work to make enough to keep body and soul together. If they got tin, so much of it went to the King, and so much for coining, and so much for the bargmaster, and there were ever fresh charges devised to be laid on them, till they cared not to work, but went away to till the fields rather than toil in the mines. Then came troubles about religion, and many men took up arms because they did not love to have their old religion taken from them—and all went to confusion. My father he married my mother, and he cared a little for the farm and a little for the mine, but most of all for the land—for he said one could live by that, but only die by the other." She turned her bright face to Eldad and said, "I weary thee with my prattle. Wilt have some more milk ?"

"I thank thee, I have enough to eat, but my ears are hungry for thy words."

"Then I must say now that on the night that I was born my father had a dream. He dreamed, and behold ! a little pyxie came to him, and he had an old face and white beard and snowy hair, all under a red-pointed cap set about with conies'

skin; and he wore a little doublet with a leathern
girdle about his loins. He had on one shoulder
a pickaxe, and he stood and looked and winked
his small eyes at my father. He said to him,
'Thou hast been in the same ball where I have
worked, but I work far, far in—where thou never
camest; and thou art a wise miner, and dost not
work to waste as do some, but art ever thrifty.
Therefore, I love thee. But it is long since I
have heard thy pick. Now, I tell thee 'that this
night there is born to thee a little maid, and
never another child shalt thou have. And once,
as thou wast going to thy work, there was a long-
cripple (adder) coiled about in the entrance to an
old burrow, and in that burrow lived my woman
and my children. They could not come out
because of the serpent, and the air was poisoned
with his breath, so that they were nigh on death.
But I was not at home, but at ball, and knew not
of it; but thou didst smite at the long-cripple
with thy staff and didst slay it. Thereby the life
of my woman and my little babes was saved.
And because of all this——'"

"But tell me," interrupted Eldad. "Did thy
father recall nothing of having done this thing?"

"Of a surety he did. He slew a long-cripple
in an old burrow, but he wist not that a pyxie
family lived in the old mound."

" Tell on thy tale, Lemonday."

" So the old man said further to my father in
his dream : ' Because thou art a true and honest
miner, and also because thou didst save my wife
and children from the long-cripple, therefore I
will do something for the child born to thee this
night. Go thou to the old ancient mine, and take
the hazel rod in thy hand, and when it turns thou
wilt find an entrance to an adit known to no man
save only to us good folk. Go therein without
fear, and ever bend to thy—nay, I cannot recall
whether he said the right or the sinister hand—
whatsoever branches and ways thou lightest on.
Go on till thou comest to where the mine was
worked no further, and there wilt thou see tin
purer and richer than ever was found heretofore
in lode ; such, indeed, as was in streams in times
long gone by when men first sought for it. Only
this I lay on thee. Use to thine own profit only
so much as thou canst carry in one hand daily.
So much is for thee, and so much alone. Whatever thou findest more bring home for her who is
born this night. Swear unto me !' "

" It was but a dream of the night," said Guavas.

" Nay ; it was more than a dream. My father
often told how he awoke and had his hand up-
raised with the thumb and forefinger and middle
finger stretched out, as one who taketh an oath."

"I can believe that; nevertheless, it was but a dream."

"But it fell out after even as the good man had said, for my father went where he had been told and he found the entrance, and he entered in and pushed on his way without fear, but with a great wonder—and verily—he came where were tools cast down and spalls of ore that had been dug out, even as the last miners had left them. But when he laid his hand on the haft of a pick-axe it went away to dust, so ancient was it."

"And the ore?"

"It was even as the good man had said."

Eldad rose, laid his hands on the girl's shoulders, and, looking her steadily in the eyes, said gravely, "Thou art befooling me, Lemonday."

"Nay; I can befool none. I am too simple. If thou mistrustest—then follow me."

She sprang to her feet and ran from the house towards an old thorn-tree that grew a little above the track leading to the door. There dense growths of bracken had lived and died, and over the soil was a tangle of its sere leaves.

"As my father came home every day from the Pyxie ball—as he called the mine——"

"Every day! Did he go often?"

"He went daily for a long while, only never when he thought any might observe him. But whensoever he returned at nightfall, then ever he brought with him a piece of ore in his hand, and he cast it towards the thorn tree. Where thou seest the dry fern, there are the stones he cast."

Eldad ran among the withered bracken, and beat them aside with his hands. Beneath them lay plenty of small lumps of stone; he picked up one, then another, a third, a fourth—all were almost solid tin from a lode.

In the greatest excitement he hasted back to Lemonday, who stood flushed with pleasure and smiling to see how keen was Eldad's interest in what she had disclosed.

" I told thee it was truth," she said.

" Where is the mine ?   I must know !" he exclaimed, impatiently.

" I cannot tell thee ; I do not know."

" And thy father—did he never work out the lode ?"

" Nay ; he brought away as much as he listed —enough, he said, for me when I came to need it.   Thanks be to God, it is not yet."

" And has no one else been to—found this— worked it ? "

" I cannot say ; I think not.   My father would have spoken out had he discovered that another had lit on the Pyxie ball."

"I must even try it. Let me carry this to the fire."

"Do as thou wilt; an' it pleaseth thee it pleaseth me."

Eldad carried the stones to the cottage. He heaped up the turf on the hearth, and inserted the lumps of ore amongst the peat. He took the bellows and began to blow, nor desisted till the whole mass glowed.

"See!" exclaimed Lemonday, "there is the pyxie metal."

A rill, seemingly of quicksilver, ran out of the fire and flowed over the granite hearthstone.

"It is tin! It is tin that is wholly pure!" exclaimed Guavas, bending over the rivulet of molten metal. "Verily, this comes of a Keenly lode."

"SEE!" EXCLAIMED LEMONDAY, "THERE IS THE PYXIE METAL."

CHAPTER XI

AGAIN : THE GOLD DUST

GUAVAS could obtain no further information from Lemonday relative to the situation of the old mine. She would willingly have told him, had she known. But she had never sufficiently interested herself about it to ask particulars of her father, and even had he told her where it was she might have been unable to indicate its position, as she had never been where it was situated.

"But if it be to thee a great matter," said she, " I know that my father had a parchment book bound in hogskin, wherein he wrote many things —as I have said to thee, he drew therein his new smelting furnace ; and therein also did he write concerning the Pyxie ball—where it lay and how it might be entered, and he made a plan thereof, for he was often there. My father was no common man ; he was clerkly, and could read and write."

"Where is that book ? "

"My mother hath it. I cannot bring it thee without her leave. Moreover, I do not well know where she hath placed it for safety. She esteems it highly for my father's sake."

"And your father never smelted the tin, and never took it to be coined?"

"Rarely. The good man had bidden him use but little to his own profit; moreover, my father gave up all thoughts of mining. He said that the ball might be worked when times were less harsh and charges less burdensome on the poor spallier."

After a couple of hours further spent with Lemonday, that passed as minutes, Eldad left. He had a walk of good two hours to his own home. He felt a happier man as he returned. The solitude and sadness of his life since his mother's death had been broken into. A gleam of pure happiness had struck across his path.

He purposed indeed, when able, to revisit Swancombe, but weeks and months passed without his being able to do so.

With the lengthening days came increase of work, and this became especially heavy, as he was obliged to remove large masses of boulder that encumbered his ground in the bottom below the cataract before he could reach the floor on which lay the stream tin.

His sole holidays were Sundays, and on such

days he deemed it would be lost labour to cross the moors to Swancombe, as in all likelihood the mother and her daughter would be away at Widecombe for divine worship, a walk of many miles in a contrary direction to that along which he would have to walk to reach the valley of the Strane.

Moreover, he was much harassed by the hostility of his neighbours; not by Rawle, who ostentatiously cultivated his friendship, but by others who sought out occasions of vexation—in cutting his leat, the watercourse supplying force to turn his wheel; in scattering his fuel, and destroying his washing floor when he was absent—acts of petty malignity that irritated without seriously injuring him, but which prevented him from absenting himself for long from his "pitch." Rawle was ever ready to lend assistance to remedy any mischief done him, and to promise his aid to discover the evil-doers.

By these means Dickon gradually dissipated the mistrust that had been engendered in the heart of Guavas. Now and again Guavas met Isolt; he saw her watching him at his work, or he encountered her on the moor. It was not that he sought her, but that accident or purpose on her part brought them together. And every such occasion infused fresh poison into his blood, and made him impatient to see her again.

As already stated, it was customary for the bargmaster to make periodical visits to the mines to investigate their workings. Each man occupying his own claim had an oak post set up by his hut, on which his name was painted or carved, and this was notched by the bailiff, if satisfied that the workings were properly conducted.

A miner was required at any time to exhibit his accumulation of black, *i.e.*, unsmelted tin, as well as his white tin, *i.e.*, that which had been smelted, and which was required to be made in a specified form, and to be stamped with the initials of the owner. Before Michaelmas Day every year, all white tin must be "coined"—that is to say, brought to one of the Stannary towns, where it was impressed with the seal of the Duchy of Cornwall, and a tithe of the tin was retained as the due of the Duchy. Any transgression of this rule was visited with penalties.

On account of the right of pre-emption and of tithing and of fining claimed by the Crown, great provocation for tin smuggling was given, which was carried on with more or less success according to the watchfulness or neglect of the bailiffs and to the craft ot those engaged in the contraband trade. Occasionally there was connivance on the part of the bailiffs or under officers who, for a consideration, shut their eyes to these transactions; but usually the miners were too poor to be able to make this worth their while. Where, however, several were combined as adventurers to work a large plot and to mine under ground, there they made terms with the officers of the Duchy to ease matters for them. The latter accordingly, unless strictly honest and impartial, looked with disfavour on solitarv ventures, and lent their hand to drive out the independent pitchers.

Where Stannary functionaries exercised rights or asserted them over land which did not properly belong to the Duchy, there controversies broke out, and opposition was encountered.

The tinneries in Devon and in Cornwall, in fact, formed an *imperium in imperio*. They were united as in a guild, but a guild exercising very extensive and extraordinary powers. They not only had their own courts, appointed their own stannators or jurors, had their own prison, but every tinner was strictly forbidden carrying any cause out of the Stannary courts, and of appealing beyond the jurisdiction of the Duchy officers.

This independence of the tinners made them arrogant and despotic. A remarkable instance was afforded in 1512, when the tinners, offended with William Strode of Newnham, member of Parliament for Plympton, who had made complaint that the miners were choking the rivers and ruining the ports with their refuse—then, although he was a member of a knightly house second only in dignity to those of the Courtenays and the Champernownes, and was a delegate of the borough, they seized on him and flung him into their gaol at Lydford, " one of the most hainous, contagious, and detestable places in the realm," as it was described. There they detained him for over a month.

The arbitrary proceedings of the Stannary courts became proverbial, and a poet of Devon wrote in 1630 :

> I've ofttimes heard of Lydford law,
> How in the morn they hang and draw,
> And sit in judgment after.

The penalties of transgressing the laws of the courts were severe.

A tinner who had defrauded the Duchy or the lord of the manor had his house burnt, and all his effects confiscated. One who adulterated the tin was required to have a spadeful of molten metal poured down his throat ; and one who had stolen of his brother tinner, if he repeated his offence more than once, was knifed through the hand till he tore himself free. A tinner who dared to sue a fellow tinner before any other court save that of the Stannaries was expelled beyond the jurisdiction of their court, and might never again make a pitch, and all his goods were confiscated.[1]

One day Rawle came to Guavas as he was leaving his trench.

"Guavas—now is a chance for thee," said he. "There is Moses at the blowing-house above the steps, and he has his purse with him."

"I desire not Moses, nor his purse."

"Nay, man ; be well advised afore thou let him slip away. I reckon that thy mother's burial cost thee money."

"Aye ; money is faster flung out than drawn in. It comes with a trickle ; it goes with a rush."

"And I heard say that your wheel was out of repair, and must so abide and hamper thee—as thy ready cash was expended."

"That also is true."

"Then, man—go to Moses."

"What can he do for me ?"

"Moses ! everything. I am sure that there is gold thou hast found, for we find the traces of it above the steps. We have the dregs and you the skim. Moses has what we have found, and given

---

[1] The penal code was confirmed by Edward I. in 1288. It is printed in the rare " The Liberties and Customs of the Myners," by E. G., 1649.

me in change this "—he held out his hand and showed coins of the realm.

" I don't know as to that," said Eldad, shaking his head.

" Ah ! did you never hear, friend Guavas, of the ancient minstrel they called Virgilius. He wrote some verses in praise of the Prince of Wales and Duke of Cornwall, and did publish them without his name thereto. Whereupon a ballet-maker took to himself the praise of having composed them, and received of the Queen a pretty sum of money. When Virgilius heard this then he wrote upon the palace gate in the Latin tongue—for he was a clerk, and had learned Latin from the parson of his parish—a line to this effect :

> I writ those lines upon the Prince ;
>   Another stole the praise,

to which he added these words, four times repeated :

> Thus ye, but not for you.

" Now the King and the Queen and all the nobles and courtiers were sore put to it to make out what this signified ; and the ballet-maker was called and bidden fill out the lines. He could not do it ; but then Master Virgilius appeared, and with a piece of charcoal thus completed the four lines :

Thus ye, but not for you, O birds, your nests prepare,
Thus ye, but not for you, ye sheep your fleeces bear,
Thus ye, but not for you, bees hive your honey spoil,
Thus ye, but not for you, O oxen, ploughing toil.

And I trow, had he been a miner, he would have added thereto this line :

Thus ye, but not for you, are delving in the soil."

" That is sooth," said Guavas ; " or was so—but matters mend a bit under our good Queen Bess."

" If it were not for a pinch o' yellow dust now and then, full sure, many of us would be ruined men in body and in purse, for, indeed, the work wears us out ; it consumes our health, our faculties, and our time ; and, good Lord ! it eats the very hope out of our hearts."

" That also is good truth," said Guavas.

" Then take my counsel, friend, and dispose of thy little pinch whilst thou mayest. And I give thee this good rede. The bargmaster will drop on thee unawares and ransack thy store, and if he finds gold will take it clean away."

" He will find none."

" Not if it be pressed into minted money afore he makes his visitation."

Guavas needed little persuasion to do as Rawle advised. He had not much gold—only six quills with the precious grains in them—and he was in sore need of money. The machinery of his blowing-house was out of repair, simple and rude though it was.

No tinner had any scruple about using to his own ends the little gold he found, so small was the amount generally obtained in the stream tin, whereas none at all was got out of lode tin.

Accordingly he delivered over his quills to the Jew, and did not hesitate to do so before Rawle and one of his own spalliers.

A few days after, the bailiff appeared on the Yealm, summoned a Court, tried Guavas for defrauding the Crown of the precious metal. The witnesses were Rawle and his workman. The jury was composed of rival miners of the neighbourhood, his enemies and ill-wishers. The judge was the bailiff, who refused to allow the case to be deferred, refused to permit appeal, and when Guavas, hoping to find leniency, confessed that he had disposed of the gold, sentenced him to be knifed to the post on his pitch. The sentence was carried into effect with indecent precipitation.

Thus are we now arrived at that point whereat we started in the first chapter of this tale of Guavas.

CHAPTER XII

"TO THE JUDGMENT OF GOD"

WEARIED out after the terrible strain to which his muscles had been subjected, and the agony he had endured, Guavas cast himself on his bed when alone, and fell into a fevered sleep that was broken by dreams. But after some hours his slumber became deeper, and it was with a start and with sleep-drunk head that he sprang to his feet when already it was morn, roused by the noise of voices outside his hut and the howling of his chained Loup.

He staggered forth, unsteady on his feet, with the stupefaction of sleep still on him.

His left hand, bound, was thrust into his breast. He held to the walls; he clutched at the granite door-jamb with his disengaged hand, and reeled forth into the raw morning light. His hair was matted with sweat; his face stained with the blood from his hand; fever spots, deep crimson as blood, were on his cheekbones, and his eyes were wild and burning. He was in his shirt, as he had been attached to the post, and as he had been released.

A large party of miners, with the bargmaster in their midst, were standing by the post, at a respectful distance from the wolf.

They looked with some surprise, perhaps somewhat disconcerted, upon Guavas.

" What ! hast thou cut thyself free, mate ? " asked one of the miners.

" Thou'st been too hasty," said another. " We would have set thee free now, after thou hadst endured the night."

" Thou wouldst free me now against the law, as thou hast condemned me against the law," said Eldad hoarsely, staring round on the men. His blood was molten with pain.

" Against the law," sneered a stannator ; " it stands writ in the constitution."

" It stands writ in the old one, maybe," retorted Eldad. " But I have oft heard that the Charter of Edmond, Earl of Cornwall, granted liberties and right to punish for all actions, life, limb, and land excepted."

" You transgressed against the Crown," said the bailiff shortly.

" Then I had right of appeal."

" Thou didst confess thy wrong-doing."

" But thou hadst no right to thus punish me."

" I am set here to do my duty," said the bailiff.

" I shall appeal—even now," cried Guavas.

"What ! against me ?"

The bargmaster's face turned pale. He well knew that his conduct would ill endure examination.

" He is right. He has been wrongfully treated !" exclaimed Humphrey Evea, who was present.

At once the tinners turned on him. "What knowest thou of the matter ? Thou art no miner."

" I say," said Evea, "that if he wronged the Queen, bless Her Majesty, she has her proper courts and judges."

This produced an outcry : " He would have appeal to the foreigners !" [1]

And one man turned savagely on Guavas, and shouted : "Is that thy meaning ? Thou wilt appeal away from the miners' courts, and beyond their liberties ?"

"Yes," answered Eldad. "But I make no appeal to the head court of the Lord Warden."

" That is well," said the bargmaster. " Look

[1] That is, beyond the Stannary jurisdiction ; to the ordinary courts of the realm.

to thyself that thou comest not worse off elsewhere. I stand on the Charter of the Stannaries; if thou appeal against me, I refuse to answer elsewhere. No foreign jurisdiction is of avail on the moor."

" It is all one," said Humphrey. "There is no Prince and Duke over you, but the Queen, and the Queen is above the Stannaries, and above the common criminal courts, I warrant you."

"Those who are under one court are not under the other," answered the bailiff. "I mock at such an appeal! No magistrate, no judge has the power to kill a flea here on our moors. We stand under the Duchy!"

His words elicited applause. None were so tenacious of their rights as the tin miners.

"Thrust him out if he dares go foreign!" shouted some men, making gestures of anger against Guavas. "He is a Cornishman; he never belonged to us."

Eldad remained unmoved. He had been considering. He could not claim redress at the Stannary High Court for the monstrous injustice done him, because Isolt had released him and had bound his hands; the bargmaster, the great offender, was her father.

He looked round on the men who gathered closer :

"I never said that I appealed away from our moors to foreign jurisdiction. I say that I do not appeal against the judgment of the bargmaster to the court of the Lord Warden. What I say is—that I do not ask if I suffered in excess of the law or not. I ask not whether the statute whereby I was knifed be in force or whether it be repealed. I cannot undo what has been done. Nothing can make my hand what it was before. But what I do declare, here and before all, is that I was betrayed to my wrong. I allow that I did sell the gold dust, as I ween, many another man has done, and he has run scatheless, whereas I come off with this——" He extended his maimed hand. "And this I suffer because I am a Cornishman, and because others lust after my pitch, and will have me thrust out of it by what means they can devise. It is true, I say, that I sold six goose-quills with some dust of precious metal in them. But I had no thought to do so; I would not have done it had I not been persuaded and provoked thereto by one who feigned himself my friend and sought only my woe. He studied occasion against me, and he found it. He laid the snare for me, and thrust me in with his hand. I appeal against him."

"Whom mean you?" asked the bargmaster,

sensibly relieved in mind that the resentment of Guavas glanced away from him.

"Whom I mean thou knowest well enough. Seek not to shelter him and to cast the shield of thy Stannary Court over him, for, by heaven, if I look not to have thee answer for what has been done to my hand, I look to him, and him I will not spare."

"Say ; whom dost thou accuse ?" asked Humphrey Evea.

"I charge Richard Rawle with having persuaded, induced, and advised me to part with the gold, and that, for his own malicious purpose, to hurt me, and for his further advancement of interest, by getting possession of my pitch here at Yealm Steps."

"I deny it ! It is a foul lie !" shouted Dickon, starting forward. Hitherto he had hung in the rear.

"He witnessed against me, having first entreated me thereto."

"He witnessed," said the bargmaster, "as was his duty. He was called thereto by the court and put on oath."

"And who told of me ? Not the Jew; he was not summoned."

"He could not be found."

"I testify and declare," said Guavas, angrily, his

eyes and cheeks flaming. "I vow and protest before high heaven that I never would have wittingly parted with the gold, had not Dickon Rawle urged me thereto by many incentives; and this I further swear, that I believe he was my betrayer and accuser. I say that but for him none would have known of what I did."

"There was thine own man, Lillicrap."

"John Lillicrap was suborned to witness. He was promised money if he would testify. And it was by Master Dickon Rawle that he was brought to speak—by him alone. I appeal against Richard Rawle."

"Dost appeal to the court I hold?" asked the bailiff, with changing hue and agitated voice.

"No; I know how justice is there sent to the wall and private interest prevaileth. No; I appeal to a higher court and a more righteous judge."

"To whom then?"

"I appeal unto God," said the angry, wronged man; and he held up his right hand to heaven.

"And how wilt thou carry out thy appeal?" asked the bargmaster with a curl of his thin lips.

"I would say, were not my hand crippled, let us fight it out between us, and he who prevails God decides that he is quit of guilt."

" Pshaw ! " the bailiff exclaimed ; " that sort of thing is of bygone times. We have none of those trials now."

" Aye," persisted the hot and vehement man, "that is true, indeed. But I ask by what fore-father's rule, old and threadbare and laid aside, was I punished ? If there was old measure dealt out to me, shall not like measure be dealt out to him ? " He pointed with his bandaged hand to Rawle, while still holding the right to heaven.

" I will sanction none of this," said the bailiff.

" No, thou wilt sanction nought but violence and wrong-dealing done in legal form. I appeal unto God against my betrayer."

" This is rank folly," put in Humphrey Evea. " Good man, how canst thou fight when thy hand is cut through ? "

" I will not maintain mine accusation myself. I will charge a friend, good and faithful, to stand in my room against Dickon."

" And who is that ? "

" He who now alone is for me—and who is impatient to say : ' Let me at him ! ' Even my wolf—Loup ! "

The proposal met with general applause.

" Dickon ! " said Evea, " if what Eldad saith be truth, then I will neither eat nor drink nor speak with thee again."

"It is false," said Rawle, angrily. "I will have none of this."

"Nay, Dickon; canst thou prove it?"

"That is for him to do."

"There is my word on one side," said Guavas; "there is his on the other. Let God decide between us."

"It shall be so!" shouted several of the miners.

"I will not! I deny it all," said Dickon.

"We have heard his charge against thee," said one of the stannators. "He saith that he did sell the Queen's gold to the Jew. Of that we doubt not. For that was he punished. But he did this at thy instigation. Let him make good his accusation as he purposes. Art thou a coward, Dickon? Art afraid of a wolf?"

"Dickon," said another tinner, "it will give us rare entertainment; better than hustling nor wrestling. Thou art a stout, sturdy man. Have a round with the wolf, and in heaven's name do not show the white feather."

"Beside," said a third, "if thou wilt not meet the beast, then we shall all esteem thee guilty, and by no other means canst thou clear thyself in our eyes. If thou didst to him as he saith, black and false is thy heart."

"And," threw in a fourth, "if thou succeed in slaying the wolf, thou canst ever esteem and vaunt thyself as the slayer of the last of his breed in England, and—" he laughed—"thou canst stamp thy tin with the badge of a wolf's head in token thereof."

"Wilt thou stand to the appeal?" asked Guavas, pressing forward.

Silence ensued. Rawle would not answer. Then some of the miners shouted out: "To the ring on Staldon! Will he, nil he, there it shall be. To the judgment of God this is committed, and He shall decide. Away with them—to the judgment of God!"

CHAPTER XIII

THE STALDON RING

WHEN a mass of men has formed a resolution, it is in vain for one man to oppose it, be he the most interested therein. The demand of Guavas met with unanimous approval, and no protests, no hanging back on the part of Rawle, were allowed.

"I shall use a cudgel," said he, sullenly.

"You shall do that," answered Evea; "but the wolf shall not wear his collar."

"I cry you nay there," said Rawle. "How shall I hold him off unless he have his collar?"

"Thou must with thy cudgel bid him keep distance," answered Humphrey.

"He shall be collared," said Rawle, stubbornly.

"If he be collared, then thou must sustain his onslaught without a staff," said Guavas. "With a cudgel it is a conflict at a distance, and with a collar it is a close grapple. Choose which thou wilt, but thou shalt not be the master in both. Whilst he ranges at a wide space thou hast the advantage; when he approaches, he feels thy strength; but should he come close on thee notwithstanding thy cudgel, then the advantage is his."

"He speaks well; it shall be so," was the unanimous judgment of all present.

Then rose a shout: "To Staldon Ring!"

And the multitude of men, gathered from all the countryside, rolled away in the direction named, drawing with them Richard Rawle.

Guavas came behind, holding his wolf by the chain.

Staldon Ring was distant to the east about three-parts of a mile. It consisted of a circle of upright granite stones, in number about one and twenty, from which leads away a single row of similar stones over hill and down dale, past cairns covering the dead of an unknown race; it overleaps the river Erme as it comes dancing from its cradle, and stretches away beyond, extending in all the length of two miles and a quarter.

Of the origin and purport of this monument nothing is known. It is not to be wondered at that it was made use of by the miners for their gatherings to discuss their grievances, or when they chose to engage in the pastime of wrestling.

Hardly had the throng of men from the Yealm Valley reached the ring before the men from the Erme appeared ; first single men running, then in twos and threes, finally in numbers, swarming up from their works, having cast aside picks and shovels. It was as though they had divined that something that would entertain them were about to take place ; yet none of the men that had been at Yealm Steps had been to summon them.

Very speedily an extraordinary concourse of men was there assembled, and gathered in a living wall around the circle.

" I protest that I will have no part in this," said the bailiff. " I hold me quit thereof."

" Ban it thou canst not. Stand and see that all be fair," said Evea. " I will lay a noble on the wolf. What wilt thou stake on the man, Hannaford ?"

" I can guess nothing how matters will fare," answered the fellow addressed as Hannaford. " Who among us ever saw a wolf tried ? Is he like a dog ? None can say. He seemeth a sorry beast, and frighted now at the many men about him. I doubt not the man will have the best in the game."

" I care not which wins," said another, "so long as we have sport."

Although others were not so outspoken, such a thought lay at the bottom of each heart.

The valley of the Erme to the present day bears extensive traces of the industry of tinners. The primeval workers had little trouble in finding the "stream tin" lying loose on the face of the rock beneath the rubble brought down by the rivers or the accumulation of peat. But with their rude methods of smelting they obtained but a poor percentage of the tin from the ore, and they cast aside the slag that was still rich in metal. In later times, when the water-wheel had been introduced to ply the bellows, then the tinners turned over the workings of the more ancient miners, and re-smelted their slag, and roasted the ore, less rich in metal, that the first men had rejected as unprofitable. Now stream-tin has been exhausted; but in every river bed, every gully, on every slope where some drainage of the hills runs, the surface has been so furrowed by busy workers as to form an unmistakable and very conspicuous feature in the landscape.

It was from these workings in the Erme Valley that now trains of men arrived running, and one might almost have thought that the line of stones set on edge sweeping over the moor to the horizon was itself a stream of granite blocks also running to witness the proposed conflict between Rawle and the wolf.

Staldon Ring had served as a meeting place so long

and so constantly for the tinners of the Erme and Yealm valleys that on this occasion the men as they crowded up took their customary places outside the circle of upright stones, and left the customary stewards, or rulers of their games and wrestling matches, to make arrangements for the expected conflict. Dickon Rawle, divested of his jerkin, stood within the circle. If he could have escaped being pitted against the wolf, he would have done so ; he looked to the bailiff to forbid the contest, but the bargmaster had shrugged his shoulders, disclaimed responsibility in the matter, and waited to see the results. He also was not averse to a little sport at another man's cost.

Rawle had sufficient knowledge of his fellow men to see that if he disappointed them in this matter they would combine in condemnation, and assume as indisputable the charge that was made against him by the Cornishman. The miners were straightforward, rough and ready men, true in word as in act, except in their dealings with their overlordship, the Duchy of Cornwall. To one another they stuck fast, and they were loyal to their privileges. That Rawle should be esteemed so base a traitor as to draw a fellow tinner into a trespass and then betray him would damn him for ever. No tinner would have any dealings with him. It was therefore necessary for him to clear himself, and that could be done only in the way offered. Old modes of thought, as old customs and old superstitions, lingered on upon the Cornish and Devon moors for centuries after they had been abandoned elsewhere. An appeal to God's judgment was, even in Elizabeth's reign, regarded as sacred in so wild a region as Dartmoor, and there was nothing strange in the thought of an appeal to a contest of force.

Dickon was a powerful man, not tall, bullet-headed, with broad shoulders and a thick-set frame. As he brandished his cudgel, it could be seen what muscles he had in his arms. He was slightly bent from working in the mines, stooping over the spade and heaving stones. His hair was short and sandy, and he had dense red eyebrows that met across his face.

Divested of his upper garment, in his shirt with the sleeves rolled back, he wore a leather girdle about the waist, in which usually was thrust a long knife. This one of the stewards removed. His trousers did not reach below the knees. They were of leather, and his stockings of thick blue worsted.

On the further side of the list stood Guavas, with his wounded hand to his breast, and the wolf at his side chained, held by his right hand.

The beast was angry, uneasy, alarmed. It had

been now many days without food, and was almost frantic with hunger. It had an inkling that something in which it was to play a part was in preparation, and was suspicious, and looked in its master's face for enlightenment.

Then Guavas with his maimed hand pointed at Dickon Rawle, and the wolf, low crouching, laid its head on its paws and growled.

The stewards came to Eldad and bade him release the beast. All was now ready.

"No collar," said Guavas. "Loup, I lay my cause on thy head. May the truth bite with thy teeth." Then to the men, "Bid Rawle swear that he did not incite me to what I did and then betray me."

" Do so, Dickon. Swear."

" I have said what I said. I will fight the cursed brute ; let him go," shouted Rawle.

Then Guavas unbuckled the collar.

The wolf looked up at him, and again the master pointed at Rawle. The beast's hair stood on end about his throat ; he drew back his gums, exposing his teeth, crouched, watched the man opposite him attentively and made a sudden rush, then a leap into the air. Rawle swung his cudgel, and the wolf hardly escaped a blow that would have stunned him had it fallen on his skull.

He dropped on all fours, turned and ran round

the circle, snarling, never for a moment removing his eyes from his antagonist, about whom he now entertained no doubt. Rawle followed him with his eyes as well, and the beast seemed unwilling to adventure another attack ; he cantered up and down, stood with one forepaw raised, and howled ; then he ran back to his master, and threw himself down beside him.

"He is a coward !" shouted some of the men. "Goad him on ! He is afraid of Rawle !"

"Loup!" said Guavas, "at him, old boy ! Look !"

The Cornishman held up the chain and collar as a threat, and the wolf, with tail dragging on the turf, crept in odd, timorous, lingering fashion round the ring, and sought a gap by which to escape.

"There b'ain't no fight in him," said one miner to his fellow. "Darned but I'm sorry I've come."

Thereupon the brute sought to find an opening ; then the spectators drew their legs together and thrust with their feet to spurn him away, and force him into the arena.

"It'll never touch him," said a man to his fellow ; "all the brute looks for is to get away."

There was something monotonous and tedious in the manner in which the creature slunk round and round the ring, and it really seemed as though it were cowed, and had no other thought than how to evade the contest.

Guavas remained immovable, undiscouraged, watching the animal as it made the circuit.

Some of those near Rawle spoke to him, and expressed their opinion that he would not have much trouble with the wolf. Others urged him to attack it, as the creature had lost all courage, and would make no resistance.

In answer to these remarks Dickon's attention was distracted, and for a moment his eye was off the slouching beast. Instantly, like a dart, the wolf rushed at him, and would have leaped, had he not as speedily recovered himself, and with a swing of the cudgel struck the beast on the side such a crashing blow that it rolled over, and lay as dead on the turf.

A roar of applause, and clapping of hands greeted this achievement, and Rawle looked round him and laughed.

" He's dead, Dickon ! You've done for'n !" was shouted.

" Now run up and knock his brains out, an'l finish'n," called another.

The wolf lay motionless, one paw over its snout, the other limbs extended stiffly on the grass.

Rawle light-heartedly advanced with his club

raised, at one blow to break the skull of his antagonist.

Guavas whistled; the brute did not stir, till the moment that Rawle was close to him, and was preparing to deal the finishing blow, when with a sudden and unexpected leap he fastened on the flank of his assailant.

Rawle uttered a cry of pain and wrath, and flung away his cudgel. The game was now at such close quarters that his weapon was unavailing.

The wolf had the wit to depend wholly upon his teeth and not to use his feet.

By running, by wrenching at the beast's throat, Dickon endeavoured to force him to let go. He beat on his muzzle with his fists; he endeavoured to drive his fingers into his gums and force them back; whatever he did he could not make the wolf let go his hold. Then he clasped both his hands round the throat and compressed them, in the hopes of strangling his antagonist. Had the wolf been furnished with a collar he might have succeeded. The beast, as it was, struggled like one that was being suffocated, but would not leave go his hold.

Borne back by the weight of the animal, and suffering acutely from pain, Dickon stepped into a tangle of coarse heather—twigs that caught his foot, and fell on his back.

Then rose a shout from the spectators of " Well done, wolf ! "

Loup instantly let go his hold, and fastened on the throat of the prostrate man.

Thereat arose a roar and a rush forward.

" Away with the brute !   It will kill him !   The game is up.   Dickon's done for ! "

Men burst through the ring and hasted to separate the man from the beast.

But the wolf had tasted blood ; was ravenous and raging.   He snapped at his assailants on all sides, sending them flying back, and returned to the throat of the fallen man.

" Kill him !   Stab him under the ribs ! " yelled some of the men.   And others cried, " Take Dickon's stick ; beat him on the head with that."

Then Guavas strode up, laid his hand on the wolf and called imperiously, " Loup ! come back ! "

The brute refused to obey.

" Have at him with the knife ! " shouted one man.

" Kick him on the head with your iron-shod boot," said another.

" Here ! " called a third ; " I'll drive my iron spud up his jaws."

And another, " Quick, for God's sake !   He's mumbling him.   He'll kill Rawle."

Eldad slipped the collar round the throat of the wolf, and lashed him with the end of the chain. Then the animal turned, and, letting go his hold, skulked between his master's feet, alarmed at the weapons brandished around him.

"Let no one touch him," said Guavas. "He has done what was required. Now he is under my protection." He drew his knife and stood over the beast to protect him. "God has judged between me and mine adversary. Spare His minister."

CHAPTER XIV

ALONG A TRACK OF CROCKS

RAWLE was lifted to his feet. His face was smeared with blood and sweat and peat mire, otherwise it was ghastly white. His hair bristled, clogged with moisture, his eyes glared with terror, and his limbs shook. He could not speak, he gasped for breath, and his hands were clutched and his feet contracted. With all the faculties of his mind fixed on the wolf, he remained in dread lest his adversary should break the chain—lest Guavas should purposely release it. He worked himself back with shoulders and elbows among the men sustaining him, as if to bring himself behind them, to interpose their bodies as screens between himself and the furious brute that had thrown him down and mangled him. The judgment of heaven had been pronounced, and verdict given against Dickon, nevertheless the pity, the fellow-feeling of the miners, was in his favour. He was the sufferer, and he was one of themselves, whereas Guavas was a stranger. They had forgotten that the really wronged man was the Cornishman, unjustly accused, unjustly condemned, tortured in a manner contrary to all law. They saw at that moment only a torn and terrified brother, scarce snatched from the jaws of a wild beast.

"What right has he," said one, pointing over his shoulder at Guavas, "to come here with his wolf ?   It bain't like a Christian, but a savage."

"Aye; if he had a quarrel wi' Dickon, why not fight it out like a man, and not send wild dogs again' him ?"

"I reckon," said a third, "that bain't a nat'ral beast neither. I've heard o' such things as devils runnin' about in animal shapes. If they helps witches to do it, why not do it themselves ?"

"Who heard tell o' real wolves at this time ? The ou'd ballad says they was all killed down by King Edgar, and I've seen that on a printed sheet as were brought to Modbury; so it must be true."

"I'll tell thee what, mate," said another miner; "I say, let us tie that there wolf up to one of these standing stones, and light a fire of furze and heather about him, and see whether he be a nat'ral beast or a devil. If he be the first, he'll burn, and well rid of him out of the land ; if he be a foul fiend, then he'll come out in a sulphurous smoke and fly away on leathern wings."

"There can be no harm tryin' it."

Guavas saw that strong feeling was roused against his wolf, and feared lest the miners should combine to wrest it from him.

He therefore withdrew, leading Loup, who snarled, and, with bloodshot eyes, glared from side to side, conscious that he was menaced, and suspicious lest he should be attacked from the rear.

Another reason urged Guavas to depart. His hand, painful before, had become inflamed, and the inflammation was running up his arm and swelling it. It did more, it invaded his head and heart, and he was dizzy, sick, and in dread of losing consciousness.

Whither should he go ? Not to his hovel, where no one would attend to him ; and he felt that he would need attention for some days till he had recovered the use of his hand—anyhow, until the anger of the wound and the convulsive spasms of his strained muscles had abated.

Then he thought of Lemonday.

He knew that he would be sure of what he needed in her mother's cottage, and at once, without debate, he turned his face northwards, and strode over the unpathed moor.

Before he had gone far a shadow was thrown before him. He might not have noticed it, and he was not in the condition to observe, when a horse forged ahead, and he saw Isolt riding. She drew rein as he halted, and she asked in her imperious tone : "Whither away now ?"

"I am going where I can have my hand dressed," he answered.

"Cannot I dress it ? Have I not done so ? Is my dressing of no avail ? "

"Your dressing was good, and I thank you for it ; but a wound demands to be attended with frequency. I cannot ask that of you."

"And whither go you to have the constant attention ?"

"I seek a woman skilled in simples."

"Where will you find one such ? "

"I have heard there is one at Swancombe."

"Oh, so you go there ! Often ?"

"I have been there rarely ; but I am assured in my mind that I shall there get what I require."

"Well, go thy way."

She turned her horse's head sharply, and rode in an opposite direction to that he took.

The consciousness grew on Eldad that sickness was gaining on him, and the one desire in his heart was that he might have strength and wit to find his way to Swancombe, a thing of which he could not be assured, as fever was gaining on him, obscuring his mind and disturbing his vision. Happily he struck on a track, and he knew it was a track that could lead only to the house to which he was directing his uncertain steps, for there was no other habitation to which it could lead. The track was not beaten by feet nor marked with ruts of cart-wheels; it was one peculiar to dwellers on the moors. It was one that might easily have been overlooked, might have been misinterpreted by an individual not familiar with the ways of the moor-men. In the Middle Ages, when the monks of Plymstock crossed the wilderness, to assure them against straying, they erected granite crosses at intervals, so that they might steer from one cross crowning a ridge to another. Many of these crosses remain, and the line is still called "The Abbots' Way." But this chain of crosses led only in two directions. One was followed when the monks of Plymstock went to visit the abbey at Tavistock on the west; the other when they directed their feet towards the abbey at Buckfast on the east side of the vast moorland. But the crosses had another disadvantage; they were no landmarks by night and in fog.

The dwellers in remote corners and dips in the hills had devised for themselves a simple and more efficacious method of indicating the tracks to and from their houses, the lines of communication between them and the great world of men. This consisted in dropping fragments of crockery— glazed in preference—at small intervals, on the turf. The success of this method was equal to its simplicity. In the densest fog it was possible to stride from one little bit of broken " cloam " to another, and at night, by moon or starlight, each glazed potsherd glanced like a glow-worm. Farmers in want of gateposts might remove a cross, and did so without scruple; but the fragments of crocks were worthless, and no one would stoop to displace them.

And now, happily for the man with clouding head, his eye caught the glitter of the fragments of earthenware running over the moss—and he had but to tramp along that line. No thought, no search of the horizon for another landmark was needed; with bowed head and eyes on the ground, he followed the shards.

As the fever in his veins and the anguish of his wound increased, he became partially unconscious, and paced mechanically, not knowing any longer whither he was going, what his object was, and what had brought him to his present pass. It seemed to him as though he were walking in infinite space, and along this space stars of various magnitudes were strewn, forming a milky way. Between them were unfathomable abysses into rayless night, into which, if he fell, he would continue spinning down the vasty void through eternity. His only hope of safety lay in treading on each star. Dimly he was aware that this luminous path led him to Paradise, to rest from pain, to repose from weariness, out of solitude into love. The chain by which Loup was held fell unregarded from his hand, and the beast followed him, dragging the links, occasionally caught by their becoming entangled with the heather, but never sufficiently to prevent him from ripping the bush up and proceeding on his way.

At Swancombe, the widow woman, Joan Ford, was sitting over the fire, and her daughter, Lemonday, was on a low stool near, knitting. The mother was engaged in spinning.

"'Twas an untoward day when your father died," said the woman. "It might ha' been a bit later, if it was to be, and then we'd ha' been rich."

"Why so, mother?"

"I reckon because he had struck a Keenly Lode."

"Will you not tell me where was that, mother?"

"Nay, how can I tell? It was a secret; he told

none, not even me. But it's all written down in the book."

"The book in the chest, mother?"

"Aye, the book where he put his plans and all. If he had not been death-struck when he was, then, as he told me himself, he would have made as much gold as would lead right over the moor where the crock chippings lie now, right away by Childe's tomb, over Foxtor to Cater's Beam and Erme Head, away and away to Cornwood. I don't mean to say there would be gold pieces all the way to Cornwood Church, but the track over the moor where marked with scat cloam (broken pottery), for every bit of scatted cloam a gold angel of King Harry, and there to cease where a roadway begins at the Moorgate by Yadsworthy."

"It wasn't to be, mother, so we need not think on't. 'Tis like countin' on the coins the old Hunter of the Wish Hounds casts to one. You take them home and find they're dry, dead leaves."

"'Tis no Wish Hunter's gold," retorted the woman; "it's a real Keenly Lode of tin, nigh pure and solid. Your father said that if it led as it bunched, he'd be a rich man, and clothe us in silk and satin."

"But father is dead, and none know where is the lode," said Lemonday.

"That's true. But it's all writ down. It will be read and acted on upon a day."

"When will that be, mother ?"

"Nay, that is for thee to find. Bring the man to me, and by the Seven Joys o' Mary I'll tell him where the lode is. That is to be thy jointure. Father made me swear it ere he died."

"Then it may lie buried."

"Thy time will come, maid. Father was a rare scholar. He said—as he was called home—that the secret of the Keenly Lode was not to be given save to him whom you should choose, and that secret is locked up in his book."

"And there let it lie locked. I want it not."

"Thou wilt change thy song one day, when the suitor knocketh at the door."

A crash and a fall.

Both women started to their feet, and looked first at the door and then at each other.

The sound had come from the door that had been struck.

Lemonday stooped to the fire, thrust in a tuft of furze that blazed up and filled the apartment with a sudden glory. Then, before the flame expired, she ran to the entrance and threw the door open. She held the flaming gorse above her head and saw a man lying on the threshold.

"Who is that ? What ails thee ?"

There was no answer.

"Mother," she cried, "bring another light. Mine is out."

The elder woman now came to the door also holding a tuft of furze that blazed.

Lemonday stooped. "Oh, mother!" she exclaimed, "it is that stranger who came here when father was lying out, and who ate his sins. He is dead!"

"He must not lie without," said the woman. "He did father a good turn."

"We must not shut the door on him," returned Lemonday, "be he friend or foe."

CHAPTER XV

ASYLUM

THE mother and daughter drew in the fallen man. He was insensible. Consciousness and power to prosecute his journey had lasted till he reached Swancombe homestead, and had deserted him then.

"By the Rood!" exclaimed Mistress Ford, "I wish Roger were here; we must have help, Lemonday; send the boy to Sherberton. Aaron Caunter must come. We must know what this means. Look to his hand—it is cut and swollen."

The girl went to a ladder and summoned a serving lad who attended to the sheep, and was already in bed. He appeared with drowsy face, and was despatched at once to the nearest farm, held by the Caunters. Mistress Ford herself was of that family, and could therefore count on assistance from her kindred. With difficulty the two women succeeded in drawing the insensible man before the fire, and they now lighted a tallow candle, whereby to discover more about him.

"What is to be done?" exclaimed the widow. "This is not a hospital that we can take in the sick, or a poorhouse where we can lodge the homeless."

"But, mother, he is our guest now. He fell on our threshold, he lies on our hearth. We cannot, we dare not refuse him our aid."

"That's like a wench," retorted the old woman. "Because he's a young man and handsome, we mun take'n in and make much o' him, and then, when he's settled in, warmed and sound, there be no tellin' what mischief mayn't come o't. If he'd been an old man, a vagabond, it would be another tale wi' you, I warrant."

"Nay, mother, don't say that. I'm not hard-hearted."

"I reckon a little too soft-hearted—and that's just it. I don't like takin' in and housin' a man as I knows nothing of—a stranger and a land-runner. What's the meanin' of his hand cut thro'? I can tell you; that's the punishment of arrant thieves. So, well featured though he may be, he's gotten a foul soul."

"Mother, you are judging him wrongly."

"Aye; I know the tale that hand tells well enough. He has come to lie on my drexel (threshold) as if this wor Lydford gaol. But if this bain't a hospital nor a poor-house, it's no gaol neither, I'll let him know."

The man lying by the fire turned, moaned, and half sang, half said, the first words of a folk-song :

" O Lemonday ! Lemonday ! thou art the flower——"

" Mother ! he knows me — he knows my name."

" But nothing else," retorted the widow. " Look to his eyes; there's no sense in them. He is off his head, sure as I'm alive."

The woman held the candle above the face of the sick man in such a manner that the tallow should not gutter over him. Then, raising herself, she said : "Go, child, and make him up a bed. There's no help for it. He might die if we cast him forth, and I doubt Aaron won't take him in as he has thrust himself on me. Bad luck to it ! and maybe the best of all will be if he die. What do I want with young men here when I've got Lemonday to watch. It's like puttin' the wolf in the fold wi' the lamb, or clappin' a butterfly into a child's hand."

Much of this was said to herself.

The woman was not unfeeling, but she was suspicious and jealous. She now bestirred herself to make a fomentation for the hand and arm of Guavas, of a herb from her garden, to which she gave the name of " Christ his fingers."

While thus engaged, the boy returned with Aaron Caunter.

" What is't cousin ? " asked the newcomer.

" See, Aaron, here's a man has thrown himself on me as is a runagate and a felon. See his hand. What am I to do—I, a lone woman—wi' the like o' him ? " She extended the wounded member, and held the candle that Master Caunter might see and judge for himself.

" This is Eldad Guavas," he answered. " I have heard of him. He has been knifed against all law and right. I know very well such things were done in times gone by, but not for many years. I've heard tell of this. The sound has gone round the country, and, if he choose, he may make some folks smart for having sentenced him. Whether he were right or wrong condemned I know naught. He's a decent conducted man, though a foreigner. You cannot turn him out. What brought him here ? "

" Nay, how can I tell ? " was the widow's answer. " He came to this house the night of my Elias's lyin' out, and he ate his sin away. I sent Lemonday to show him the track to Child's Grave, and by Foxtor mires. Whether anything passed that has made him fancy her, or she him,

I cannot say, but the only word he has said since he came in was her name, and she's been mighty hot on housin' him."

"You must rid yourself of him as soon as he be well enough to leave."

With the assistance of the widow, Aaron now lifted the insensible man, and carried him to a chamber within, up a short stair, above what served as a dairy, and Lemonday held the light whilst they laid him in the bed, and stripped his jerkin off, so as to free the arm. This had swollen to such an extent as to fill his sleeve, so that they were obliged to cut it to release the arm.

Guavas moaned, turned, but made no effort to resist, and seemed hardly to recover his consciousness, and when he did, only in glimpses, again to be clouded.

When they had done, they returned to the kitchen.

At that moment the door was thrown open, and the old man, Roger Gale, who worked for the widow on her farm, burst in, breathless. It was some minutes before he could recover himself sufficiently to make himself understood. Then he gasped:

"The rout is out, and is coming here!"

"What rout?"

"Dickon Rawle and his men!"

"What want they here?"

"They be coming after the foreigner."

"Indeed," said Aaron; "and wherefore do they seek him?"

"They say he has half murdered Dickon, he and his wolf atwixt 'em; and they're swearing to have the life of him for it. There's a party of half a dozen."

"They are coming here?"

"They be now crossing the clacker. Hush! you can hear their voices. I runned on ahead to give warning."

"Let them come," said the widow. "This is my house, and none can enter it without my leave. The foreigner is under my roof and is safe."

She went to the door and barred it with an oak beam.

"You'll not keep them out with that," said the old man. "You don't know Rawle; he'll break through."

"Then," said Aaron, "he must even pass me."

"There are some six of them—lusty fellows."

"To break into a widow's house is no light matter. God and the angels defend her. Boy! get a weapon! Roger, arm yourself!"

A shake at the door, and a shout: "Open!"

Aaron went to the little window, consisting of but a small opening in the wall, closed by four small panes of glass, and replied, "This is no tavern. What would ye ?"

"We'll tell you that when we are inside."

"Then keep your secret outside. This house has no door for you."

"Who answers ?   The Cornishman ?"

"No ; I—Aaron Caunter, of Sherberton. And you ?"

"I am Rawle, of Hawns. Let me in, Caunter. I will do no harm. I must bring forth the Cornishman, if within. You have him in shelter there ? Yes or no ?"

"Yes."

"Thrust him forth."

"By what right do you ask this ?"

"By this ; that he is an outlaw. He has robbed the Queen. He has been knifed and escaped without cutting himself free.   He has tried to murder me. I demand him."

"Are you a constable ?"

"I claim him. I will put him where he can henceforth harm none."

"Where is that to be ?"

"In Foxtor Mire."

Then ensued a lull.

Presently from without another blow at the door, followed by a shout.

"Are you going to give him up ?"

"No."

"You will not give him up ? You harbour the outlaw—the felon ?"

"He is no outlaw. As for his felony, who tried ? who convicted ? By what law was he sentenced ?"

"Come !" shouted Rawle outside. "Break open the door, lads."

"Stand back !" ordered Aaron Caunter. He took down a long sword that hung on crooks above the fireplace; it was that which had belonged to the deceased, the husband of Mistress Ford. The boy produced a muck-fork, and the old man armed himself with a cudgel.

The beam was strained in its sockets as the assailants dashed masses of granite against the door.

Then a piece of the planking gave way, and next a stone in the wall started. Some of the men had brought a log of wood, a post taken from a shed, and they swung it as a battering ram against the valve.

A crash, and the woodwork yielded and fell in.

With a shout of exultation those outside rushed forward to invade the house. The widow kindled furze, and filled the room with light, so that the intruders could see that they would be opposed, and that, too, by a man wielding a sword.

Nevertheless they pressed in, and though not advancing far into the house, yet were beneath the roof and within the doorway. Aaron Caunter drew back so as to guard the stair. His little company was inadequate to hold the entire kitchen against the assailants.

"Come, now," said Dickon Rawle, who appeared with face and throat bandaged, and streaks of blood on his cheeks. "Look you, Aaron Caunter! I wish to do you no ill, nor will I touch Joan Ford, nor her daughter. Stand back, and let me through. I will, I swear by Heaven, have that fellow out, and sink him in the bog. See how his devil has mauled me. It is his familiar. He is a warlock, and we will rid the country of him."

"Show me your warrant," returned the moor farmer, "or you do not come forward another step!"

"I swear," retorted Rawle, "I will not leave this place till we have got him. We will not go back till we have finished what we purpose. He has a meere down at Yealm Steps, and by his witchcraft he bleeds our meeres, draws all the gold out of our tin, drains our tin away. He, the Cornishman, spoils us. And then—he sets his devil, in wolf shape, on me to mangle me. By Heaven, I will have him in my hands!"

" Stand back," said the widow to her kinsman. " It is my place to speak with Master Rawle. I tell thee, Dickon of Hawns, that this is my house, and that you have committed felony yourself in breaking in. There be witnesses, and I call on all to stand by me when I summon thee before the Queen's High Court to answer for this night's work."

" I'll answer," scoffed Rawle, " never fear. The Queen has a long arm, but her hand hardly rests on Dartmoor. We are in a duchy here, and make our own laws, and carry them out ourselves."

Then Lemonday appeared, descending the stair.

" I pray, I pray desist," she said. " You may push on, and pass over these our defenders, but you'll have to tread me underfoot or ever you mount this stair."

She descended, and thrust past her mother and Aaron, knelt in the space between the assailants and the defenders.

" He whom you seek is ill; he cannot speak; he is as one dying—on his bed. Will you fight against, carry off, murder the sick ? "

" Hear, hear ! " laughed Rawle. " He has cast his witchery over the maid, has this Cornishman ! Look to 't, Mistress Ford."

He moved forward to thrust Lemonday aside,

when Caunter swung his sword, and the intruder sprang backward from its sweep.

A mass of burning peat fell, and the fire shot up lurid, filling the whole apartment with a vermilion glare, lighting the faces of the men who stood in the doorway, and the pale, blood-smeared features of their leader.

Then, in the doorway of the sleeping chamber at the stair-head, appeared Guavas in his shirt, haggard, with a glassy look in his eyes. He held the jamb and looked down, unable to understand what was occurring, unconscious where he was.

At that same instant, through the little open window plunged the wolf, and planted himself in face of Rawle, his hair bristling, his fangs gleaming in the firelight, and his eyes glowing like carbuncles.

The apparition was so sudden and so terrifying that the intruder at once fell back. The men behind him gave way, then turned and ran as they would have run from no man.

In another moment not one was within the house.

CHAPTER XVI

THE PARCHMENT BOOK

SEVERAL days had passed, and now Eldad
was somewhat recovered from the fever and
prostration that had ensued after his knifing,
and the excitement which had followed.

He had been kindly and constantly nursed by
the good woman, Joan Ford, and by her daughter.
Whilst delirious he had talked of the tin streaming
incessantly, and of the gold-dust found with the
tin.

One evening the mother and Lemonday were
seated on the bench before the house. Eldad
Guavas had gone forth on a ramble, and they
were alone.

"That was a rare feat of Loup to chase a
covey of men the night those fellows broke into
our house," said the girl. "Roger tells that the
wolf went round them in the dark, snapping,
baying, making rushes at one or the other, and

they swore they were attacked by a legion of
wolves. But it was only Loup; in the night
their fears made them fancy he was a whole
pack. Roger went after them behind, and he
saw them, huddled together, scrambling up the
hill, every one afraid to be left by himself, all
turning to fight off the beast whom each reckoned
was assailing himself. It was a sight to make
him laugh, so says Roger. And all this went on
till they reached Childe's Cross, and there Loup
let them alone. I warrant they have made a fine
May tale out of this. But, indeed, they hold
Loup to be naught else but a war-wolf. He is
tame enough with you and me and Roger. He
has the sense of a Christian, I reckon."

After a pause, Lemonday proceeded, "What
do'y think now, mother? They've behaved
shameful to him, have they not? treated him as
if he were a proven criminal, and all for naught;
he has done no wrong."

"You know nothing about the matter," said
Mistress Ford.

"I've heard Cousin Caunter speak, and Roger
Gale."

"Yes—you've heard one side."

"But sure, mother, you don't take that of
Dickon Rawle, as broke into our house, and
would ha' killed 'm."

"I take no side at all.   I have heard only what is rumoured."

"And what have you a mind to do about Rawle ? Be you going to summon him ?"

Mistress Ford shook her head.

"What good would that do to me ? He might be punished, or he might not. He has friends and kinsfolk as 'ud make me suffer. I know that Caunter be for it, but I have no wish to stir in the affair. He has done me a wrong, and if I push in the matter, I may bring down a score of others on me, and behind all stands Rodda, the bargmaster, and he's a dangerous man to have as an enemy."

"And all considered," said the girl, "they came off the worse. They broke open our door, that's true, but they did no other harm, and it will not be in a week that the laugh will cease against him, for the tale will go abroad of the six men running and tumbling one over another all the road from Swancombe to Foxtor mire, because they were deadly afeared of one wolf, that's no bigger than a great sheep dog."

"We're feeble and they are strong," said the widow, "and it is best for us to bow to the storm and let it pass over our heads."

"I reckon the best way to punish such as Dickon Rawle is to help on Eldad," remarked the girl. "For some reason he's mighty bitter against Master Guavas."

"He is bitter against him, because he was brought to shame through him in the fight at Staldon Ring. Guavas appealed to God, and God fought for him and declared Dickon to be a liar and false accuser. I wish the sick man were well out o' our house. I don't want to be brought into these quarrels. I thought here in Swancombe we were well out o' the current of mortal strife, and it seems we're gotten into the eddy."

"I don't see how Eldad can return to Yealm Steps," said the girl. "He'll go right into a hornet's nest."

"That is his affair, not ours."

"Nay, mother, if we can help him out, without hurt to ourselves, in the name of heaven let us do it."

"How can we do it."

"Why, mother, what does the Cornishman look to but finding a good pitch? He has had trouble where he was. Shall we not help him to another where he will be away from his foes?"

"What do you mean, child?" asked the mother, turning her face aside, so as to hide from her daughter the embarrassment painted on it.

"I mean, mother dear, that we might tell him

of the pixie lode, of which father spoke so often at the last."

"Of the pixie lode?" repeated the widow. "That is all a fable."

"Nay, mother, for sure it is nothing of the sort. It is all truth as the naked Gospel. Go and bring out the parchment book in the locked cypress box, bound in pigskin. There are some pages in it, nigh the end, on which father made a plan, so that one can easy find the entrance to the adit which leads to the lode. So long as he lived, right enough it was that we should keep the secret, because, I reckon, he thought to work the lode himself, and come to great riches, so as to pave the way wi' gold from Swancombe to the Yealm; or he would ha' done so, but for that he had passed his word to the good folk who rule in the ball. But now he is gone where no lodes can be worked, and no tin profits."

"The lode and the tin may profit us who remain," answered the widow, sharply.

"How can they, mother? Neither of us be miners."

"There is Caunter."

"He is no miner. He will be rich in sheep, and naught else. Every man to his trade."

"There may come another who will work it."

"There need come no other. God has sent the man to us that we require—Eldad Guavas."

The mother had been considering what to say and do.

" Pshaw ! " she said, " it were naught but a dream o' your father's ; a fairy tale, and a bit o' brag. There's naught in the book about it."

" But mother, you yourself told me there was. You—the very night when Eldad came to us."

" I were telling a fairy tale, and nothing more ; just as we old women love to do, to amuse children. It's none but children as believes these silly tales."

" I am sure it is in the book, mother. I pray you go and fetch it."

" I'll bring the book, if you list, and if you find it there, then I will give you a new gown at Michaelmas."

So saying, the widow rose, and laying aside her distaff, entered the house.

She went with trouble in her face to the stair, ascended it—the stair was winding, of stone, in the depth of the wall—and, entering the bedroom occupied by herself and her daughter, opened the long spruce chest that contained her festival garments, and such treasures as were hers, and were most carefully guarded, a couple of silver skewers for the hair, a prayer-book, a necklace of drilled pieces of crystal, and a stone axe-head, or "thunderbolt," as she called it, that had been dug up on the farm, and was regarded as a preservative against witchcraft.

From the bottom of the chest she drew her late husband's notebook in its pigskin cover. A peculiar expression came over her face, indicative of satisfaction that by her wit she was able to forestall any mischief that might be done by the artlessness and inconsideration of her daughter—and a real mischief that would be, to disclose to a stranger the secret of the lode, and it were a betrayal of a sacred trust as well.

Mistress Joan Ford had spoken of the discovery, and had allowed her tongue to run away with her, when amusing her child with dreams of future wealth ; she had been encouraged to this by her husband, whose brain had been excited by his discovery, and by schemes how to make the best of what he had found with advantage to himself, and not to others. But Elias Ford had been afraid to do too much lest he should contravene the injunction he fancied had been laid on him by the pixie, and partly lest he should excite the cupidity of others, and the treasure be taken from him by connivance with the bargmaster.

When he was attacked by his illness this discovery had been on his mind, and he had made his wife promise not to reveal the secret save on such condition as was laid down in the book. She regretted that her daughter knew of the book, and of what was in it. She had unfortunately told her of this—now she must make provision that no use was made of this communication to their common disadvantage.

Having the note book in hand, she went to the little window, seated herself in it, and opened the book, which was tied with strings passed through the edges of the cover.

Near the end was what she sought; and she read with some labour the words there written by the failing hand of her husband. She was not much of a scholar; what little she knew she had been taught by her husband. She could spell out words laboriously, and so now she deciphered what he had inscribed in the book as the expression of his last wishes :—

I give and bequeath my soul to Almighty God, and my body to Widicombe churchyard. The house and farm of Swancombe is not mine ; it belongs to my dear wife, Jane Ford : it is hers, and I have never concerned myself more than was needful about it. I have ever been a miner, in heart and soul. It has been my good fortune to discover an almost pure lode of tin, and I believe it bunches. This discovery I give and bequeath to my only child, Lemonday, that it may become her marriage portion ; and I constitute my beloved wife Joan sole executor and administrator of my wishes ; and I desire that she shall not give up the secret of the Keenly Lode to any one other than to him who shall become the husband of my daughter, Lemonday, and that, only on condition that he be a miner. But and if he be a Moor man or farmer, then shall my wife, Joan, reserve the secret, and only communicate it to our daughter, Lemonday, on her death-bed, and with the condition that it shall be delivered over to her son, should he become a miner, or to her daughter, should she marry a miner ; for to what end is it to tell a farmer of a lode ? He will value it as little as a miner will a heap of dung. This is my last will and testament, in the name of the Father, and Son and Holy Ghost. Amen.

I add hereto a plan and description whereby, without fail, the lode may be found, and I desire, should the lode be worked, that it be entitled " Wheel Lemonday."

Joan Ford's tears flowed as she picked out the meaning of these lines, and then with a sharp knife she deliberately cut out the page, as well as that on which was the plan with description, and hid these pages in a side box for ribbons and tapes belonging to the chest.

Having done this, she descended with the book in her hand, resolved to persuade her daughter that she had been cherishing a delusion.

When she came outside the house door, she found Guavas there, speaking to Lemonday, and in great agitation.

CHAPTER XVII

A CLAIM LOST

ELDAD GUAVAS had taken advantage of recovered strength and of a fine day to revisit his claim or " pitch " at Yealm Steps. He could not walk with vigour, his powers were greatly reduced, and the way was long ; but with resolution he pursued it, till he came out upon the fall of rock over which the river bounded to the place where he had been accustomed to work, and which he considered as indisputably his own. To his surprise, and indignation, he found the " meeres " invaded. His working ground was alive with miners engaged in turning over the rubble brought down by the stream, in " vanning "—that is to say, sifting with a shovel—and in " stamping," crushing the lumps so as to extract from them the tin that was mixed with quartz and micaceous iron.

In towering anger he plunged down the steep

hill side, and ran into the midst of the workers. With flashing eye and flaming cheek, he stood amidst the men engaged in examining the gravel and broken stones.

The process adopted by "streamers" was this. They began at a low level and worked upward. They collected all the rubble, broke it as small as possible, almost to powder, and then tossed it in the air on broad shovels, when the wind "fanned" away the quartz, and left the metal on the shovel; or else they did the same in water, where the current could carry away the earthy particles; and this was done again and again, till a warm red dust appeared on the broad surface of the shovel, and this was nearly, if not wholly, pure tin.   Occasionally a golden particle was distinguishable in the dust, and this was eagerly secured.   But gold was rare.

As the men proceeded upwards they built a culvert behind them of granite blocks, through which the water might flow away, and then buried this under the rubbish rejected as they worked further. To the present day the furrowed remains of ancient stream works scar the surface of the moor, and the stream runs away through its artificially constructed channel deep under the moss and grass-grown rubble piled high above it.

When the streamers became doubtful whether

their run of ore was likely to continue, they threw out advance pits called "prospecting" or "costeening" holes, and carefully explored what was brought up from the depths below. An ancient working can always be recognised by its advance pits; even though the main works are now so overgrown and overlapped with turf as to bear all the appearance of natural gullies.

Such stream works were carried on upon the surface. No mining was done in them. But in addition to these there were a few genuine mines, with adits driven into the bowels of the hills; hitherto these had not proved very remunerative, and till the streaming operations had exhausted surface tin it was hardly necessary to go below, and at great cost to follow vein tin. Another reason beside cost told against mining proper. Stream tin was absolutely pure. It could be melted in a peat fire, and would run out as a bar of silver, wholly free from obnoxious elements. It was other with vein tin. This was never pure, but mixed with sulphurets of arsenic and iron, which rendered the tin brittle as glass. Accordingly, to make vein tin serviceable, it had to undergo a double process, the first a delicate one, the roasting, to expel the sulphur, and then the smelting. Consequently the acquisition and preparation of tin from underground mines was vastly more costly and laborious than streaming. The latter was carried out by individuals, taking meeres or claims ; the former could only be executed by companies.

"Why are you on my pitch ?   What right have you here ?" gasped Eldad.

One of the miners turned his head over his shoulder, and answered : "Be that you, Guavas ?"

"It is I ; and I have come to ask what brings you here.   This is my claim."

"Be it ?   I reckon I heard you'd not renewed."

"It was renewed."

"How might that be, when you was pinned to the post, and hadn't a hand wherewith to cut a turf ?"

"It was cut for me."

"Who did that ?"

Guavas could not answer.

"If you want to put in your claims, you must prove them.   When a pitch is abandoned by one man another steps in."

"What ! Guavas here !"

The call came from the bank above.

The Cornishman turned and saw Isolt mounted on her black cob.

"Come here ! I will speak with you," she ordered with her wonted haughtiness.

He obeyed.

Eldad reached the top of the cutting, and stood beside her horse with his hand on the crupper, looking up into her beautiful face. She fixed her large, maddening eyes on him. At once, weak, enfeebled by sickness, perhaps because of the returning sap of life, the rising tide of health, he felt a thrill of passion run through his muscles, and that the blood in his veins began to leap and boil.

"For what are you here?" she asked, without withdrawing her eyes from him.

"Why should I be anywhere else?" he answered. "I have been ill—in fever and off my head. Now I am well, and I return to find that I am robbed. They have seized on my meeres. They deny my rights. They have occupied all my claim."

"You did not cut your sods and establish your claim."

"I could not. You know that very well. You did it for me."

"And for that reason the pitch is mine. They are working on my rights, and by my orders. But tell me, what have you done with all the tin and the gold that were on it? We have found nothing."

"This claim yours! You have defrauded me! I did not think that of you."

"My good friend, do not blame me. If I had not claimed, the meeres would have been taken from you by others. There were a score on your ground as soon as you were gone, and it was thought you had not renewed. I stood forward, pointed to the turned sods, and swore that I had preceded them all, and that the pitch was mine."

"And so it is you who rob me ?"

"I ? I hold it for you."

"Whilst I have been absent, see how the spalliers have been turning over everything. There will be nothing left for me."

"They have found but little. How is this ? Are you, as they say, a warlock, and have drawn the metal after you ? The men are disappointed. They tell that you went away with your staff, and dragged the end along the ground, and that the tin ran after you in a molten vein all the way, and has left behind nothing but gozen."

"That is foolish talk. I told you that there was little ore to be had here."

"Yet you found gold ?"

"Aye ! by a piece of rare fortune that recurreth not every day. The luck ran together, if you will have it so, but when it came into my hands turned like pixie gold to misfortune. Had I not found the gold, I should not have suffered as I did."

He held up his maimed hand.

Isolt made a gesture of impatience.

" How is it that whilst you are here there is a yield, when you are gone there is none ? "

" How can you be sure there was a yield when I was on the pitch ? "

" Everyone said so."

" Everyone said it because everyone fancied it, and all because of those few unfortunate grains of gold."

" I have heard you made a gold-washing machine."

" I made a model in zinc. When I discovered the gold particles, I believed I was about to find more. Then I contrived such an apparatus as might readily sift out the metal, but it never passed beyond being a model. That has sufficed to set men's wits wondering and their tongues wagging."

" It is my belief," said Isolt angrily, and she struck the horse unintentionally that it leaped and nearly rolled down the gully, and would have precipitated the girl to the bottom had not Eldad thrown himself in the way.

" What is your belief ? " he asked when Isolt had recovered her balance. He held the horse by the bridle, and looked her straight in the face.

" It is my belief," she said, " that you have

drawn away all the metal after you. What are you doing at Swancombe?" she asked fiercely. "Why are you lurking there—laughing at us, I wot—as we search for the gold and find none."

"I say to thee, I went there to be nursed. I was ill. There is tin in the stream, but I do not suppose that there is much gold."

"No, you have carried that off. And of tin—there is not much."

"I never said there was. I told you the contrary."

"This is witchcraft!" she exclaimed angrily.

"Yes," said he, "this is witchcraft, but it is not in me, it is in thee. You have been playing with me a cruel game—you have your belief, and you will hearken to naught I say."

Her lip curled. She said nothing, but turned away, and Eldad retraced his steps to Swancombe.

Eldad made his way over the waste as quickly as he could; his heart, his mind were in a turmoil. Isolt Rodda fascinated him. He loved her—he believed that she was fond of him. Had she not released him from his terrible torture that night when he had been transfixed to the post? Did not her eyes tell him that she loved him? Did she not seek him out? And yet, he was doubtful. If she sought him, was it for himself or for the gold and tin he was supposed to have found—for the

secret of finding the ores he was held to possess ?
She had even now taken advantage of his absence
to secure his claim, and she was exploring it in
such a manner as showed vast eagerness to discover
its value, and in a fashion generally condemned
and indeed illegal.

He reached the paddock before the house at
Swancombe as Mistress Joan Ford issued from the
door with the parchment book in her hand.

Lemonday hastily took it from her, ran her eye
through it with some excitation of mind, that
increased as she discovered that what she sought
was no longer there. She returned the note-book
to her mother with a questioning, almost pene-
trating, glance. The marks of pages cut out from
the end, precisely where she believed the plan had
been, had not escaped her observant eye.

"So it was all a fable ? " she asked.

"It has that look."

"And I had so great a wish to give Master
Guavas a pleasure. See, mother, he seems more
than ever discomposed now."

"You can't give pleasure to every Jack who
comes to our house."

"Oh, mother ! He is a worthy man and has
been ill-served." Then, as Eldad stood before her,
she rose, and, with heightened colour, asked : "You
have been far ? "

"I have been to Yealm Steps."

"And have found there all in order?"

"I have found everything taken from me."

"How so?"

The tired, disappointed man seated himself on the bench and related what had taken place. The indignation of Lemonday was great. Her generous heart took fire.

"It is unjust!" she exclaimed. "This never can hold."

"It will hold till the whole claim has been turned to tails—that is worked over by the spalliers, and nothing left worth having. I have not forfeited my pitch. I could reassert my right to it. I could not lose it by default of a day; but what am I, to maintain my just rights against the many, against the bailiff's own daughter? Might is right on Dartmoor and within the Stannary Bounds, for all the decrees of the Duchy and the laws passed by the Courts."

With flashing eye Lemonday sprang up, took Eldad's wrist, and said, vehemently: "Follow me!"

She led him forth from the yard in front of the house to a bit of broken ground covered with bracken and furze.

"Look," she said, "look! Do you remember what I showed you before, among the bushes?"

"Yes, there are tons of tin here."

"They are yours!" she answered, triumphantly. "My father gathered them for me. I give them all to you."

CHAPTER XVIII

MISTRESS JOAN FORD was angry with her
daughter.

"Why did you speak of this?" she asked.

"Oh, mother, forgive me. *This* was no secret
hidden away in a book. Father talked of this
openly, and he used to say every day he had
brought me another spall to my fortune."

"My daughter, Lemonday," said the widow,
addressing the Cornishman, "has done what she
ought not to have done. She has told you of this
heap of spalls. It is hers——"

"Then, mother, I give it to Eldad Guavas,"
interrupted the girl.

"Listen to me," said the elder woman, in a tone
of great annoyance. "If you have any honour in
you, you will not touch it. It is hers, that is true,
but she is a child, and does not know the value,
and she has no right to give away this collected
store of tin."

"How comes it here?" asked the miner. "This is no outcrop of ore. This is no stream bed. Every bit is a spall and has been brought."

"You are right," answered Joan Ford. "Every bit is a spall and has been brought."

"But who brought it?"

"My husband, who is with God. Every day that he returned from where he worked, he brought back in each hand a spall as big as he could hold in his fists, and before entering the yard, he threw a piece on one side. And he ever said that there would then be something to fall back on in an evil day, and there would be something to set up Lemonday when she married."

"Your husband brought all this! But where did he find it? Whence this comes there, there must be more—a lode the like of which is not in the West."

"Where he got it I do not know," answered the widow reservedly. "I cannot say that it all came from the same ball."

"It did—that is to say—most of it did," said Guavas. "I can tell that by the look of the fragments. They're all samples from one lode."

"Wherever that was, I do not know. Elias went out o' mornings and returned at fall o' day. I never went with him——"

"But did not Lemonday?"

"No," answered the woman sharply. "Lemon-day had other things to mind than to go to ball."

"Did he never tell you where it was ?"

"If he told, I did not give heed, and have not carried what he said thereon in my head."

"But—such a find—it must not be lost. It will be the making of the man who comes on it."

Mrs. Ford offered no reply, but bit her lips.

"Where this comes from there, there must be more."

Still no answer. Lemonday took her mother's hand and looked pleadingly into her face.

"I know nothing more about it," said the woman in a tone of annoyance, and drew her hand from her daughter.

Eldad considered for a moment, and then said, "Mistress Ford, it is of no use letting all these spalls lie here. Did your husband never bring them to the blowing house ?"

"He had no blowing house of his own and there was none nigh. But he did now and again get some smelted."

"He was bound by the Stannary laws to do so regularly, and now I strongly urge you to allow me to put up an oven and turn all this black into white tin, and so convert into money what now lies idle. If you do not so, and a strange miner comes this way prospecting and casts an eye on what lies here, he can at once claim and carry off all this store. You have made no use of it, and the laws require the conversion into white tin, and forbid the hoarding of black ore."

"You may do as you propose, and welcome," said the widow, "but mind you, the tin is ours, for all that we have not roasted it."

"I am not ungrateful for what you have done for me," answered Guavas. "I was a stranger and ye took me in. I was sick and ye ministered to me. I shall never do other than what is for your profit. The tin is yours, and I will account to you for every ounce. I will work as your man, and you shall pay me wage, if you will, till this entire accumulation is smelted up. All I ask is that you will suffer me to do—what I have a right to do—range the country and seek out the place whence your husband got all these pieces. The place at Yealm Steps is lost to me. I have too many enemies there to seek the same grounds again, and moreover it will all have been spoiled. I must find fresh quarters."

Joan Ford was uneasy and disconcerted.

"Let us consider that another time," she said. "Now think only of the blowing house."

"That will not be a hard matter," said he. "You have one already below you, at the sweep of the river——"

"What, Lower Swancombe?"

"I do not know its name, but there are very ancient workings there, and among them the ruins of a blowing house, small, but sufficient; and I shall have to restore the furnace, and roof the building, and with small trouble I can put up a wheel and have a blast."

"You will not be false to us," said the widow, nervous, mistrustful, hesitating.

Guavas smiled. "Mistress," answered he, "you cast on me the sins of your husband, and who can say but that all the pains, the injustice, the persecution, the robbery, to which I have been subjected since that night, that these, which have left me maimed and impoverished, may be the expiation of some of the sins, the sufferings that ever follow on sin? If I have borne these, then let me bear some of the obligations, the privileges of the dead man, and work for you—his widow, and for his daughter."

"I must e'en trust thee," said Joan Ford, "for I cannot help myself."

"You may trust him because he is true," said Lemonday, with beaming eyes.

The tinner smiled.

"I will go and see the old blowing house," said Guavas. "I shall look on it now with other eyes than heretofore."

As soon as he was gone, Joan Ford seated herself on the bench before the door and signed to her daughter to take a place beside her.

She did not speak for some minutes, so great was her agitation. She had her hands in her lap, and she plaited the fingers together and unwove them, to again re-plait them—a sure token to Lemonday that her mother's mind was in commotion.

At length she had sufficiently established control over her features and voice to speak. Then she said, without turning to Lemonday :

"You did wrong, very wrong, to show those spalls to Guavas."

"Oh, mother, it was no secret."

"It was not like the secret of the Keenly Lode, that I admit, but it was not a thing to be told to any one."

"Mother, Guavas is not *any one*. He is a true man, and good. He has undergone sore mishaps, and I would do everything in my power to make him happy."

"Do not thou set thy baby head on making of men happy. Men cut and hew their own happiness out of the rocks for themselves, and the woman who comes in their way offering it gets no thanks, and is cut and hewed down before them. Women expect happiness to arrive as hailstones out of heaven. They hold out their laps, and get them full. Not so with men. They must win it with pick and fanning shovel, with crusher and with fire blast. Happiness they value not otherwise. To us it is precious as coming unsought ; to them only as quested and found."

"Mother, he will melt up those stones, and give us the money. And if he should find a lode or a run of stream tin near here, why should we begrudge it him ?"

"I do not grudge it him, so long as he does not light on——"

"Then there is that lode father spoke of."

"If there be—he must not find it. If there be not—nothing is lost. If there be, it is not for him."

Then she pressed her daughter's hand, and took it to her, and laid it against her heart.

"Lemonday," she said, "now that thy father is gone, I have none to think of, none to love but thee. As to my old bones, fain would I lay them beside thy father's in Widicombe churchyard ; but my time is not yet come. Thou art too foolish, too fond, to be left unguarded. Look me in the face, Lemonday."

She turned her head, and the girl raised her honest eyes to her mother's, and gazed steadily into her orbs.

"Lemonday, thou'rt nineteen years old to-morrow. Too old to be still a child, too young to be a woman. Think of the vein of pure tin of which thy father spoke—that is hidden, that is precious, that is desired by so many, but which is only for him to whom God reveals it. Such a vein of precious metal every maid has in her. That is her heart's pure love—unmixed and marred by wolfram—it is her honour, it is her pride, more precious than life and fortune. Do not trifle therewith. True heart's love and self-devotion in a maid can be revealed to one, and to one only, in the whole round world. Remember that. If trifled with, if shown to all, if not kept sacred and secret for the one to whom God giveth it—then is it but the tailings left such as the spalliers cast behind their backs, scornfully. As in a stream work there is tin, and he who digs there first raises the precious metal and profits by it, but he who comes after has naught but refuse, so is it with every maid. Her vein of pure ore, and there is none without it, is for the elect of God who finds it, and marks the bounds and saith, 'Behold, now this is my pitch, so help me God.' With whomsoever thou goest, whether among the poor spalliers or the farmers, or should chance to stand among princes, it is all one—keep the precious vein for the elect one—all the rest is tailings."

Lemonday's eye did not sink. She smiled, leaned forward and kissed her mother's lips.

" Be without fear for me," she said.

"I am not without fear," said the mother. "Thou art prodigal. First thou wouldst have the book and open it before this vagrant man ; and then thou didst lead him to the spalls thy father cast one by one, through many days, for us, and not for this stranger."

All at once both started back in fear. They saw a shadow, they heard a voice : " I have found it— I make my claim ! "

Before them stood Eldad Guavas with his hand uplifted, and a forked stick between them, above the head of Lemonday.

" See ! " said he, almost with a shout, " the Dousing rod turns and points. I have found the precious ore—it is in her."

As he had returned from Lower Swancombe in the twilight, under the yard wall, he had heard some of the words spoken by Joan Ford. He had drawn from his bosom the divining rod of hazel, which he ever bore about with him, and standing unperceived by the women, engrossed in each other and in their own thoughts, had held the rod above the girl's head, and verily it had revolved in his hands, and the head had pointed downwards to her.

" I make my claim," he said again.

CHAPTER XIX

THE BLOWING HOUSE

FOR a fortnight Eldad was engaged at the reparation of the old blowing house. It was an oblong building of small dimensions, with a pit at the side in which still remained the oak wheel that had formerly worked the bellows. These ancient wheels were small, rarely over four feet in diameter, and were provided with leather buckets to their paddles. The buckets had long ago disappeared, but the paddles, made of bog oak, black as coal and hard as iron, were uninjured. Indeed, this blow house had been abandoned within the memory of Joan Ford, when the stream works in Swancombe had been left exhausted. The "leat," whereby water was led from the river further up the valley to the wheel, remained, and needed but little clearing out. A fresh "launder," or wooden trough, had to be constructed and set in place for conducting the stream as a shoot into the buckets of the wheel.

The walls of the structure were of granite blocks, and six feet thick; they were sound, and needed but to be roofed over at the top with a few beams and thatched with rushes.

The furnace was of the simplest construction. It consisted of a circular barrel of stone lined with clay, communicating by a chimney through the wall with the outer air. In the elbow of the chimney much tin was often deposited, and raked out when the furnace was cool.

Bellows were rude, constructed with boards and leather, the latter of home production, the skins of the beasts killed on the farm.

The reparation of the blowing house awoke great interest in the mind of Lemonday, and she often took her spinning or knitting down the river to the point where it swept round a spur of grass on which the ruin stood. There she sat working, singing, conversing with Eldad as he pursued his self-imposed task.

Every now and again the mother came that way, suspicious and unwilling that her daughter should be so much in the company of the Cornish-man ; she also would stay, if the weather was fine, in the sheltered nook of the folding hills, with the prattling river at her feet.

Nothing further had been said by Eldad after his declaration that he made a claim on Lemonday, and the girl and her mother regarded his words as a joke.

Ever since the memorable night in which the wolf had chased away Dickon and his followers, the beast had kept apart. It had obtained freedom when its master dropped the chain. It had succeeded in breaking the chain; and having once acquired its liberty was resolved to maintain it.

This was unfortunate, for the wolf became a terror to the flocks and a danger to the farmers in the ancient tenements on the moor and its neighbourhood. When hungry, Loup helped himself without scruple, more often, indeed, in the warrens among the rabbits, but not infrequently among the sheepfolds, and took his toll of the flocks. This occasioned complaint and remonstrance. Guavas was unable to recover control over his unruly monster, and prevent him from continuing his depredations. That Loup would fall a victim in the end was inevitable, but it would be a difficult matter to pursue and bring him to bay in the vast and untrodden wilderness, full of refuges among rocks and under bracken.

Guavas dared not light his furnace and begin

operations till he had registered the blowing house in the books of the Stannary Court. Accordingly he had to appear before the bargmaster, and announce that he had constructed a furnace and that he was about to produce white tin.   .

The announcement caused great astonishment, and was widely commented on. He had made no claim to a pitch in the Swancombe valley. Whence was he to procure the tin he would run into moulds ? That was his affair, he answered. There were no stream works in the neighbourhood. There had been, but they had been exhausted. Indeed, old stream workers' "burrows" had been turned over there within the memory of man, and resifted and reground, and nothing worth taking away had been left. His demand to have the Swancombe blow house registered could not be refused; and he was bidden preserve his old letter for the tin he sent to the Stannary mints. No tinner or smelter was allowed to sell any tin which had not been assayed and impressed with the duchy arms at one of the Stannary towns on the borders of Dartmoor. And none might sell tin, whether black or white, without paying the dues of the duchy. They might not even dispose of the clinkers or dross from the furnaces without a warrant, lest in so doing they should fraudulently dispose of the precious metal—tin, from which the Crown derived so large a revenue.

Another custom had to be complied with—not legal, but enforced by usage, that of inviting all the nearest smelters to the "christening" of the new furnace. Had this usage not been complied with, they would have contrived to wreck it, and there would have been no redress obtainable at the Stannary Court.

It must be understood that at the time, and the same applied to earlier ages, though there were regular courts, officers, laws, and customs appointed for tin miners—yet, to a large extent, these men were a law to themselves. The Crown interfered merely for the purpose of maintaining its rights, of protecting itself against fraud, otherwise it left them to do pretty much as they pleased. An act of severity in protection of the Crown rights, or those alleged to be such—like the unwarrantable transfixing of Guavas to a stake—was certain to be winked at, and appeal against the officer who had ordered and executed such a judgment would have been passed from court to court, delayed hearing from one term to another, till it was forgotten, or the appellant wearied out, or dead.

Guavas had discovered among the ruins the granite blocks, in which were cut the old moulds for tin ingots, imperishable relics of the period when the industry was carried on in every valley. To the present day these moulds remain, and where the blowing houses are reduced to mere mounds overgrown with heather and fern, these tell the story of their purport and former importance. But he found more than the moulds; he found the receiver of the molten tin, a slab of granite with a spoon-shaped excavation in it. This formed the basis of the furnace. As the ore became red hot, it distilled tin, which dropped in silver tears through the fire into the bowl below, and ran out when the c'ay was removed which stopped the mouth of the kiln, and ran down the channel into the moulds prepared to receive the stream.

In preparation for the " christening," Joan Ford had killed a sheep, and had provided two kegs of "white ale," a brew at one time next to cider, the most general drink in the West.

Andrew Borde, in the first half of the sixteenth century, described this tipple as :—

> " Smoky and ropey
> And never a good sope."

And of the Cornishmen he says : "This ale is stark naught, loking whyte and thycke, as (though) pygges had wasteled in it."

It is made of grout, malt, and eggs, and has a white, curdled, and not very inviting look. The secret of its composition has long been preserved in certain families. If likely to perish shortly, mankind does not lose much.

The day of the "christening" was one of fog, when there exists extreme difficulty in finding the way over the moors. Accordingly, only half-a-dozen blowers arrived at Swancombe, and, instead of feasting out of doors, were obliged to crowd into the hut, where meat, bread, and ale were served out to them by the Cornishman, after that the furnace had been heated.

"Where d'ye get your ore?" asked one of the blowers; "seeing as how you ain't got no pitch."

"That I may answer," replied Guavas. "I have a store of the making of Elias Ford. It is not my own. I am doing the work for Mistress Ford."

"Let's look to it," said another blower, and Eldad readily showed him some lumps. These were passed from hand to hand.

"Well, now," said the first blower, "I ought to know the looks of that. I've seen none like it on Dartmoor, saving and excepting what Elias brought, and where he found it he never told."

"I reckon," threw in another, "it weren't so terrible far off from Chaw Gully."

"What d'ye mean by Chaw Gully?" asked a third, named Coomin.

"Why the ould Roman mine as is haunted."

"Drat them hauntings! I don't believe nothing about 'em, Philip French."

"Don't you?" retorted the man addressed by the name of French. "No more did Roger Rawle, the brother o' Dickon. You've heard o' he?"

"Yes, but I never heard no sense of it."

"Then you're in the same state as others. Roger, he swore that the ore was gotten out o' the Roman mine, and he'd go down and see. You mun understand as how there's a shaft walled about; nobody dun understand how deep it be. They say o' a frosty mornin' there's smoke cometh out o' that shaft, as though it were the chimney to hell fire. But as for an adit to that mine, none ever saw any."

"Well, and what of Roger Rawle?"

"He said, said he, he didn't care a deuce for spirits, and he'd go down a shaft and see if that were the place whence Elias got his spalls of ore."

"He went down?"

"I reckon he did—and Dickon, and he, and

Petherick Lillicrap was in it. They'd got a
windlass, and Roger were a main daring fellow ;
so they let him down."

" Well—— ? "

" And as they looked down—they saw—both of
'em will swear to it—a hand and arm come out
o' the side wi' a knife and cut the cord."

" Cut the cord !   What cord ! "

" The cord by which Roger were lowered down
the shaft.   Aye ! they was that struck wi' fear,
they couldn't draw up nor let down, and all at
once up ran the cord slack.   And where Roger
fell to God Almighty only knows."

" Did not they go down after him ? "

The narrator laughed drily.

" I reckon," said he, " you'd ha' thought six-
teen and a half times afore you'd have done that.
What if that spirit hand had come out again and
cut the cord by which you hung ?   No, for very
surety, Dickon may have axed Lillicrap to go
below, and just as sure Petherick replied :
'Thankye kindly, Dickon, but it's your brother,
not mine, has falled, and so won't you descend
and fetch him up ? ' "

" So—the body was not recovered·? "

" It was—and that's another coorious thing
about the whole tale."

" How was that ?   Who went down ? "

"Nobody went down. The dead body came up o' its own self."

"That is not possible."

"It was so. I promise you there was a rare commotion about what had fallen out. The family said they couldn't let Roger Rawle lie there unburied, and some said they'd fetch the priest from Widecombe to bless the shaft, and say the burial service over where he lay. For, for sartain, no man would go below, and risk to run the same chance. The next morn—what should folk see, but the dead man lying stretched out at the head o' the shaft all along on a gozen burrow. They'd nothing to do but carry the corpse away and bury it."

"How do ye account for that ?"

"I don't account for it noways. But some say that as this was an old heathen Roman mine, and the spirits had taken possession of it, that they couldn't abide the presence of a Christian man among them, and they cast his body up. Not but there was need for them to be so mighty particular. Roger Rawle weren't much to brag of as a Christian. But how was the spirits to know that ? They bide down in the bowels of the earth, and don't concern theirselves with what goes on above. I reckon they saw the cross of baptism marking him—and so they kicked 'n out."

"Well, that's a wisht tale," said Coomin. "It's not I that would care to go down thickey shaft—not if there were gold at the bottom."

"I reckon it's easy enough going down," said French, grimly; "it's the coming up again is the difficulty."

"And that was in Chaw Gully. Where be that to?" asked Coomin.

"Don't you know the Webburn river? It's not the West Webburn; it's nigh on what is the King's Oven."

"I know the King's Oven well enough."

"There's a raven nests there right over thickey Roman mine," said the narrator of the tale. "I've heard tell that this same raven were there when William the Bastard conquered old England, and will be there till the crack o' doom. Some folks tell it be the very raven as Noah sent out of the Ark, and which never came back; but I can say nothing as to that. When she croaks then the spirits below are bidden be on the look out, for Christian men draw nigh."

"Mates!" shouted Eldad, who had been unnoticed whilst the discussion proceeded relative to the ore and whence it came. "Mates," said he, "I will tap the furnace!"

Then he took an iron rod, and with a loud

cry of "Joseph to the tinners' aid!"[1] he drove
it into the clay plug that closed the mouth of
the kiln. At once a brilliant silver stream
gushed forth, poured through the runnel, and
rapidly filled the mould, overflowed, and ran
on into a second that communicated with the
first by a channel.

The men, looking on, exclaimed: "By the
Lord! that's old Elias's tin and no doubt.
There is none other like it on the Moor."

"The heathen tin that came out o' Chaw
Gully," said French.

---

[1] Now corrupted to "Joseph was in the tin trade!" One
Cornish tale is that this Joseph was he of Arimathea, that he
made his fortune out of tin, and that on one occasion he
brought the Child Saviour with him in his boat to Cornwall.

CHAPTER XX

FRIEND OR FOE

THE blow house men were gone; and dusk had settled in. But with the set of day the pall of vapour had lifted, and a ripple of saffron light had run over the upland region, leaving basins and creeks of purple shadow between the hills, in which listlessly wandered whisps of fog that had lost their way.

Eldad sat musing by his furnace; before him lay the tin in its moulds gleaming with the light that shone in at the little window, and looking like two pools of quicksilver. The metal was slowly cooling, and the ingots could not be turned out of their moulds till next day. He was musing on what he had heard.

There could, he surmised, be little doubt as to whence Elias Ford had brought the tin. If not from Chaw Gully, it must have been from somewhere near there. From whatever place he brought it, the exact position of that place was unknown to the adventurers and single miners on the moor ; they thought Elias Ford obtained his supply from the old Roman mine, but they were not certain. None had seen him enter it. All they had discovered was that he took the direction of this mine every day.

Elias had no recognised claim anywhere. Had he been engaged in streaming, he would have been discovered, for a work in which tin is washed clouds the river and colours it red, and thus betrays to all below what is going on in the stream above.

Elias, apparently, had found a subterranean mine, and had worked in that. Indeed, the spalls that Eldad had seen were of vein tin and were not surface ore. This had been obvious to him from the first, and he had calcined his lumps to expel the sulphur, before submitting them to the smelting furnace.

He concluded accordingly that the tin was from a mine. Now a mine can only be worked by a company—such a company was in those days called a Society of "Adventurers." Elias had not formed one of a company. He must therefore have either found an outcrop of ore on the surface, easily workable without burrowing, or he must have entered and followed some ancient mine, and continued the old works that had been long abandoned.

Another matter connected with this train of thought obtruded itself on his consideration. He had been not a little surprised at the resistance offered by Mistress Ford to every suggestion that she should summon Dickon Rawle before a magistrate for having broken into her house. He knew sufficient of the woman's character to be sure that she was one to resent an injury with vehemence, and not to rest satisfied till she had exacted the utmost punishment for a wrong done her which the law would afford; but, although a flagrant outrage had been committed, she would not allow any steps to be taken to bring Rawle to justice for his misdeed. When Caunter almost insisted on her taking proceedings, she manifested first hesitation, then an alarmed shrinking back, and finally assumed an attitude of sullen opposition. It was in vain for her cousin at Sherberton to point out to her that this was no case for a Stannary Court in which a miner would be well supported by his fellows, and in which he might hope to carry all before him. Rawle would be brought before a common justice of the peace, and tried by the common law of England. No representations were of avail; to all Joan Ford turned a deaf ear, and clothed herself with an impenetrable panoply of dogged resistance. For this there must be a reason, and Guavas was led involuntarily to connect this with the circumstance of the death of Rawle s brother in the Roman mine.

What was the explanation of the hand stretched forth with a knife that cut the rope by which Roger hung? Eldad put from him the supposition that this was supernatural. That the rope had not been cut by a projecting piece of rock was certain, for, in the first place, the shaft was walled about, and therefore could have no rugged protrusions ; and, in the second place, Dickon and another, looking down the well, had distinctly seen the arm protrude from the side. This might have been the fancy of one man, but hardly of two, at one and the same moment. Was it possible that Elias had been at the time in the mine, not at the lowest level, and that he had deliberately cut the cord and precipitated Roger to his death to prevent the discovery of that precious vein of tin which had been discovered or revealed to him ? If so, did not this also explain the bringing up of the corpse, and the laying it near the opening of the shaft, so as to obviate attempts to descend for the purpose of recovering the body. One difficulty stood in the way of this explanation, and that was—how had Elias Ford himself got down into the mine ? The answer to this was that he knew of some opening other than the shaft by which access to the ancient workings was obtained. No wonder, if Mistress Ford were aware that her husband had killed Robert Rawle, that she was averse to a feud with another of the same family, that she was willing to pass by a deed of violence committed by Dickon, because she was aware of a crime committed against Roger, his brother, by her own husband.

Eldad started up, went outside his blowing house, and was grasped by a hand. He looked round and saw Isolt, in her black cloak, the hood drawn over her head. The fog had damped her dark tresses, and streaks of hair protruded and hung over her breast.

"I have come to speak with you," she said, in a quivering, passionate voice. "You have been false to me ! You have not done what you undertook."

"How so ?"

"I made you mine when I drew the knife out of your hand. You swore to be mine."

"In all things honest I am so still."

"In all things honest ! Do you doubt my honesty ? Honest !" she repeated, in a gasp of scorn. "Oh, you pious, canting knave ! A thing must be honest, or you will none of it; and yet all the while you are in league with Beelzebub, and he teacheth thee how to draw after thee all the veins of fluid mineral. Say the truth, thou hast left never a drop of tin behind, and not the finest pillum (dust) grain of gold. Yet were both at Yealm Steps whilst thou were there. As thou didst dig thou didst recover the metal. Now that thou art gone there is none. As I said to thee, I would work the place for thee, and thou and thy devil-master, in the shape of a wolf, have played a game with me, and befooled me. Ye have sucked it all away, to draw it out here—here," she thrust in at the doorway and pointed to the ingot moulds, filled and brimming over with shining metal.

"There!" she exclaimed, "you have a well-spring of tin—as the Israelites had a rock that followed them ever bubbling with water, so have you a vein of ever flowing metal that runneth and throweth up drops of gold along with the other and less precious metal. Wherefore have you led it away from me—to keep it all to yourself?"

"You are mistaken, Isolt."

"I am not mistaken. See there! at the first christening—there is the outgush of the vein."

"This is metal, but not of my raising.'

"Who rose it, then?"

"It was raised by the husband of Mistress Joan Ford, who is dead."

"So—you are working for her!" said the girl angrily. "You are false, false to me. You are my man. You swore to be mine."

"I will be true and faithful to you, as I swore."

"You lie! You are false. You have gone into her service. But come now. We will treat together. Be it so; thou art with her, and without ever asking my leave. It matters not. Whence got her man, who is dead, this store of tin? Find me that out, and we will work together and be rich, thou and I."

Eldad laughed. "You work!"

"Aye! I can manage on my side without hands. Am not I the bargmaster's daughter? Cannot I contrive matters with my father to our twin advantage, when I see the way, and have a trusty friend with whom to work?"

"You mean—that I am to spoil the widow for your profit."

"I care not how you put it. See here, Eldad," she seated herself on a stone, and knitted her fingers about her knee. "I have taken a vast interest in thee—Cornishman though thou art. I know not wherefore. I have done so ever since we were together at the Crockern Hall. And I was ill at ease with myself, for my father fain

would give me to Dickon. When I saw thee at
the dance beside him, by heaven, I said, I will
have none of Rawle, and if I must take a man, it
shall be this dark stranger. But the man to wed
me must be rich or I will none of him. And when
I heard of thee, that thou didst wondrously at the
Yealm Steps, and got gold out where others found
nothing, and hadst thy familiar spirit to point out
where to dig and turn over the gozen, then I
thought thou shouldst be the man I would have.
And next I heard how thou hadst been caught and
sentenced against all law—to be knifed to thy
stake. And my heart was on fire. I came, as
thou knowest, and set thee free, and bound thy
hand, and took from thee an oath not to belong
to any other but to me, that I might do with thee
just what I would, make of thee my servant in all
things."

"Nay, I never swore to all that."

"Thou didst give thyself wholly and unreservedly
unto me."

"Well, what wouldst thou have of me ? What
wouldst thou do with me ? Speak now, that I
may know thy will, and that I may answer. For in
very truth, after my ability, and up to my measure,
I am willing to fulfil what I have undertaken."

She paused before answering, looking at the
ingots. She had thrust back her hood in the hut,

as the furnace and metal in cooling gave forth much heat. Her dark, wild locks were tossed about her shoulders; some fell over her face. She put up her fingers and thrust them back behind her ears, then resumed her clasp of one knee.

"I will be thy friend through life, or thy deadly enemy. It is so with me. I feel my heart is full as that mould, and full with as hot a load. I know not whether it be love or hate. It may be either, if it run this way or that. Tell me, why art thou here—with the Fords, mother and daughter?"

"I can answer freely. Because driven away from Yealm Steps."

"But why go to them?"

"Because I knew none other to whom to go."

"Thou shouldst have come to me." Then, after another pause, during which she rocked herself from side to side, looking at him with eyes in which was a phosphorescent gleam, "I do not like thee to be here. It must not so continue. There was ever strange talk of Elias Ford—that he had found pixie tin. And now—you say this is his ore you have been smelting. Who gave it you?"

"Mistress Ford."

"Then—thou knowest whence it comes."

"I do not know."

"Find out—and when thou knowest—come and tell me, and I am thine."

" Is this thy purpose ? "

" Yes. Find out whence this wondrous tin comes. Question thy familiar. The wolf will go about with thee, snout to ground, and scent it. But I mistrust thee. Thou hast the secret already —that baby maid has told thee all."

" Indeed, I have not the secret."

" Then watch, and slack not till thou hast found it, and thereafter, when thou hast won it, ask of me—to be thine own. See." She put forth both her hands. " I will take thee to my heart. I care not that thou art a stranger—with my father's help we will cozen folk all round, and become rich as princes."

" I cannot do what is required of me."

" You will not."

" Be it so. I will not."

She looked at him steadily from under her dark brows with eyes that flashed fire.

" I understand thee," she said between her teeth, " thou hast come here, drawn by that fond maid Lemonday, and think with her to share the pixie tin. I swear 'fore God thou shalt not. I will not be mocked or flouted and cast aside for a milk-faced quean. What can'st thou do against my father and me ? Think of that."

"I desire not to slight and be against you or your father."

"You must be one thing or other; be mine and fling the net and draw the moor and all its tin for me—aye, and its gold to boot, and have me; but I swear that I will not endure to have my offer thrown back in my face ·Which is it to be ?"

"I cannot betray those who have been good to me."

"Then—come ! I understand thee. We are no friends, but enemies—to death !"

She rose, without another word, to leave the blowing house.

"Stay !" exclaimed Eldad, going after her. "Give me back my promise. Set me free."

"I cast you from me—you are free; and woe betide you thereat."   And, plucking his ring from her finger, she threw it in his face.

CHAPTER XXI

AGAIN: THE WOLF

WITH labouring bosom, flaming cheeks, a
scintillating eye, Isolt ascended the steep
slope of the moor above the blowing house.

She was wrath, disappointed, and jealous.

Isolt was well aware that her father stood in a
position of peril. His reckless misuse of the
powers entrusted to him as bailiff, the way in
which he had dealt with his opportunities to his
own profit, not in the interest of the duchy, or of
the miners, his veniality, his trickishness, had
stirred up hostility on all sides, and it was
generally known that his delinquencies would be
made matter of complaint at the next Stannary
Court ; when, unless he were able to clear himself, the loss of his office would be the least
punishment he might expect.

Isolt had heard that the Cornishman, working
at Yealm Steps, was either endowed with extra-

"

ordinary luck or was possessed of more knowledge than the other miners. Rumour exaggerated his success, and represented him as rich.

Hearing this of the man, she was predisposed to be interested in him when she met Eldad at the dance, and then, when she saw how finely built and handsome he was, her fancy was caught, and she exerted her powers of fascination to capture his heart.

She had many admirers, notably Dickon Rawle, to whom her father had given encouragement; he was not dependent wholly on what he found in streaming, for he had a small yeoman estate on the confines of the moor.

When her father had sentenced Guavas to be fastened to his stock by a knife thrust through his palm, he had himself suggested to his daughter that she should release him, as he was alarmed at the prospect of what might happen to himself should the man tear his hand away and become crippled for life. In releasing him, Isolt was to exact of Guavas that he should make no complaint of the manner in which he had been treated, and that she should bind him to herself, so as to be able to use him, or reject him as proved expedient.

And she had encountered disappointment in the working of the claim that Eldad had owned

and where he had found the grains of gold.
What gold there was he had carried away, what
tin was there had been in pockets which he
had emptied, leaving none behind.

No sooner, however, was this Cornishman
driven from his pitch, than he found another
source of wealth, and that one apparently vastly
richer than the first. If she could have maintained her hold on him at Swancombe, and have
got him to betray his trust and extort from the
Fords the secret of the source whence came the
pixie tin, then all would have been well. But he
had rebelled against her control, he was fallen
under the influence of another woman, and Isolt,
as a woman, could not forgive such a lapse.

Cold of heart, yet passionate, without love that
is tender, but with resentment that is cruel, she
was resolved to throw herself into the arms of
Rawle, if only he would help to discover the
secret whereby both might be enriched, and in so
doing revenge her on Guavas, who had slighted
her proffered affection. She was well aware that
at one time she had obtained a hold on the Cornishman's heart, and she was now confident that
she had lost it. This she could not forget, nor
forgive.

The weather had changed. The day had been
one of driving fog and rain. Towards evening

the mists had come together into a lumbering black cloud that hung over the high ground to the west, and gave to the setting day an angry scowl. The vapours were piled up of pitchy darkness, and pulsated with electric flashes.

On reaching the summit of the hill, Isolt found Dickon Rawle standing by her horse. She had, in fact, left it under his charge on the high ground.

"An ugly night," said he, "I mistrust me that we shall hardly reach shelter before the storm break."

"I have spoken with Guavas," said the girl, regardless of the weather; "and, Dickon, you have often said you desired my heart—here is my hand. It was once stained in his blood, but that was when I sought to save him. Dip yours in it, to avenge me, and our hands shall clasp. So only shall it be. He has offended me past forgiveness."

"Faith now?" said Rawle suspiciously. "I have occasion against him, but thou——?"

"If thou and I make one, then it must be that I know thee to be no pitiful knave who has borne a drubbing and dare not resent it. I will have to man only such an one as proves himself to be a man, and has put his foot on the neck of his enemy. Understand that."

"Give me but the chance, and I will not spare him."

"Find the chance. It becomes thee not to stand looking round thee, helpless, till it come. Find it for thyself. A wrong done thee should sting and burn like a nettle, till the sting and burn be quenched in blood."

"That is true," answered Rawle. "I have no desire but to close the account that is betwixt us, but—I must be wary lest in thrusting him over the brink he draw *me* along with him into destruction."

"Find thou occasion, if thou hast spirit, and when found use it as a man."

"That I will do assuredly."

"Yet, first, Dickon, it behoves thee to discover where his luck lies. When he was working at Yealm Steps, there was ore in plenty; when he left, the ore deserted the claim. Now he is here at Swancombe, the metal comes flushing every vein like rising sap in herbs in spring. How does he contrive this? If we could wrest his secret from him——"

"There is no secret," answered Rawle. "I have e'en been speaking with Coomin and others, who have been to the christening, and they say he is working up old ore gotten by Elias Ford."

"Is that so? He said as much to me, but I doubted he lied."

"He said it to them.   They were sure of it by the appearance of the mineral.   They said they could take oath it came from Chaw Gully."

"Then let us speed thither."

"What, now ?   To-night—with a storm brewing ?"

"Nay, I am no such fool.   If he got the tin from Chaw Gully, why not you or I ?"

"He has not gotten it himself from that place. He has what was brought away by Elias Ford in time past."

"Then let us forestall him, and make our claim."

"Nay—do thou.   I dare not.   Know you not that it was in the Roman mine that my brother met his death ?"

"I heard that thy brother fell down an old shaft left unclosed."

"We held that Elias Ford got this wondrous rich ore from the Roman mine at Chaw Gully. There is a shaft open in that place—there may be more for anything I know to the contrary.   I have seen but one.   It is walled about, four square ; that shaft goeth down none know how deep.   Roger and I had found that out by watching ; and one day when we thought none saw us, and that Master Ford was not there, Lillicrap and I let Roger down.   But he never came up alive."

"An accident befel him—but thou mightest be more happy if thou didst venture."

"I shall not venture. No man will venture there now. I tell thee, Isolt, Lillicrap and I were looking over the edge as we let Roger down, and we heard him shriek such a shriek as I never heard man give afore. Then we looked further and beheld an arm issue from the rock at the side, and it did hack with a reaping hook at the cable, and never rested till it had cut through the cord, and Roger fell—God knoweth whither. Nothing will ever make me think of descent there. If Guavas venture and bring up treasure it is well, let him do so, and we will carry off his spoil, against that I say no word; but descend myself I will not—nor will any other man who fans tin and hath heard of what befel my brother."

"Thou'rt certain he gets the ore thence?"

"I know only that Elias Ford produced such ore as was seen in no other hands, and he would tell to none whence it came. Then Roger and I watched, and we saw him some twice or thrice enter the Gully."

"And descend the shaft?"

"Nay, we were not near enough to see that."

"I tell thee, Richard," said Isolt, "that this Cornishman will forestall thee here as he forestalled every one at Yealm Steps. There he came and reaped the rich ears and left but the stubble to the rest. It will be so again at Chaw Gully. He will not be baulked by pixies and hobgoblins, but like a brave man will face them. They are shadows——"

"By heaven!" exclaimed Rawle, "that was no shadow which cut the rope by which my brother hung."

"Thou wilt see," pursued the girl, "he will dare do what thou shirkest. He will gather where thou holdest back thy hand. I will not have thee, white liver that thou art. I tell thee now is the time that he must be brushed out of our path lest he get all the wheat out of Chaw Gully and leave us, as he did at Yealm Steps, naught but the bran. The metal is there, thou sayest, and so say also the rest. How long is it since Elias Ford died?"

"Not many months."

"Well, and in all this time there has been none with heart stout to defy the pixies that guard the mine. He—this Guavas—has no craven fears. You or he must make the claim. If he claims—then thou hast naught but the old scrapings and scum as afore—gleaning as a goose in arrish. Put thy hand to't at once boldly, and it is thine. Tarry, and it is lost to thee for always."

"I cannot go down the shaft."

"I do not ask that. Certain is it that the treasure is in Chaw Gully. Thou art too fearsome to venture for it. Then, in God's name, is Eldad Guavas to have it?"

"Not so, by my troth."

"Then prevent him from going there. As yet he has not been to the Roman mine; but as surely as ever the store brought by Elias Ford is done, so surely will he start to raise more. If the treasure be not thine, shall it be his?"

"By mine honour, no!"

"Then go at once and avenge thy wrong. He is still at the blowing house, but he will speedily be on his way to the house of the Fords. Let it be your care, Dickon, that he never again cross the threshold alive."

Rawle hesitated.

"I will tarry for thee here," said Isolt. "Hast a knife, or must I lend thee one? Must I spur thy dubious manhood?"

At that moment both heard the mournful baying of a beast. At the same moment the landscape was illumined by a flash of lightning, and in the blaze they saw the wolf run by—black against the flame—but with eyes turned on them and fangs that gleamed in the evanescent flash.

Rawle drew back, the horse plunged and snorted.

"The brute is still at large," he said. "The thought, the sight of him makes my blood clot in my veins and my marrow freeze."

"Let thy blood thaw, then, and flow—take this knife and go—bring it me back red in the blood of the wolf's master, and so shall I know thou art a man."

CHAPTER XXII

BOUND AND RELEASED

ELDAD was not in the blowing house when
Rawle reached it, stealthily approaching
and listening at the door.

No doors were locked at that period, at least,
on Dartmoor. When people desired to hide
anything they made for themselves *caches*, or, to
use a Cornish word, fogous, excavated caves in
the indurated gravel, or built-up chambers under
rocks. Such are to be found in considerable
numbers still on Dartmoor, and others are being
occasionally lighted upon by accident.

When Dickon had made sure that Guavas was
not in the workshop, he thrust open the door and
entered. Within, the chamber was hot and dark.
He struck a light and kindled an end of wax
taper he carried with him, and examined the
interior.

The newly run tin glittered, reflecting the ray
of his candle. He looked at it with covetous

eyes. Then he searched for spalls, pieces of unbaked or uncalcined ore, and found a pile in the corner. He seated himself on a bench and closely examined these. His practised eye assured him that they were composed of tin almost pure, with but little spar and micaceous iron, perhaps a third of the whole might be dross—the rest was metal. His greed and envy were excited. The Cornishman, driven from his diggings on the Yealm by his means, because he was envious of the success of Guavas, had transferred his operations to this remote spot, and had come on ore far richer than any found where he had worked previously.

Rawle, like the other men who had examined the spalls, was convinced that the specimens came from the old Roman mine in Chaw Gully, but how they had been extracted thence was beyond his wit to discover. There was a mystery connected with it, and with the solution of this mystery came a certainty of wealth.

He leisurely left the blowing house and made his way to Swancombe Farmhouse, and having rapped at the door, entered.

The widow and her daughter started in surprise and alarm.

Rawle held up his hand to allay their apprehension.

"Fear me not," he said, and seated himself on a bench by the table. "I wish you no ill, nor bear any malice for the events that are past. Nay, I am ready to allow that I intruded, and that with violence, where I had no right to be. But Mistress Ford, consider the provocation, that I was mightily aggrieved and angered with my wounds, and that I had good occasion to pursue the foreigner, Guavas, who had put me to open dishonour. See," said he, exposing his throat, "the scars are there even now, and will mark me to my death day. Wherefore didst thou harbour him ? I had good cause to come after him. But now I am here to make reparation for forcibly entering thy premises. Tell me at what price thou esteemest the injury done thee, and I will make good and we shall be friends."

Joan Ford remained silent, looking into the fire.

"I have made no complaint. I have not proceeded against you, Richard Rawle," she said, after considering for a while.

"I know that it is so, and out of mine own free will am I come to offer restitution. I would fain be on good terms with all, and chiefly with thee."

"And why chiefly with me ?"

"For that thou art a widow woman, and I will not willingly have it said of me that I came like a night thief and broke up thy house.   I did it in a time of great provocation and anger, but I had no desire to offend you, and therefore I now come to offer an explanation and to make amends."

He unloosed his belt, and drew forth a purse. At the same time he laid a heavy pistol on the table.

" What hast thou there ? " asked the widow.

" It is a pistol," answered Dickon.

" And for what purpose bearest thou a pistol ? "

" I have good cause when a wolf runneth wild on the moors, and that one from whose bites I have suffered and am marked.   E'en now, or ever I came here, I saw him, but had not time to shoot."

The widow, more interested in the firearm, then somewhat of a novelty, took up the pistol and examined it.

" I bid thee be wary," said Dickon.   "The barrel is charged, and that with a silver bullet. I reckon lead availeth not against a hell beast such as the wolf.   Therefore have I cast me one of silver.   If I had not seen Guavas and the wolf together, I would have said that the man was a warlock and changed himself at pleasure into the form of a beast.   But I am very assured that the wolf is his familiar.   Who ever heard of wolves in England for a hundred years and more ? "

"Nay, I have heard of them, but not in this part. He saith this beast came out of Cornwall."

"It came out of the nethermost pit of Apollyon," said Dickon, resuming the pistol. "And if I see either the wolf or his master, I will try the efficacy of my silver bullet."

"Go thy ways," said the widow, "I will have none of thy money, and I desire not thy presence any further."

"Where is Guavas ?" asked Dickon. "I have sworn vengeance on him, and before I return home I will fulfil what I have sworn."

"Go forth—thou ruffian !" exclaimed Joan Ford angrily, "thou'rt come a second time to my house for the same purpose. Has the eternal Lord God forsaken thee ? Art thou rushing on destruction like a mad dog, forgetful of thy honour, thirsting for blood, to bite and mangle ? Go forth from my peaceful house ; I will have no dealings with a man who carries such thoughts in his head."

"What ! am I to go forth into the wild night ? See how it lightens ! Hark, how it rains ! It is dark on the moor, and how could I find my way home ?"

"I care not. Go into any outhouse ; here thou shalt not abide."

"Whilst Joan Ford spoke, Lemonday drew the

pistol from the table, and giving it to the small serving boy, bade him take it out of the kitchen.

Dickon saw the action and sprang to his feet.

"Give me my weapon," said he. "Are you thieves here?"

"I will not leave the pistol with one who will use it for violence," answered the girl.

"Return it to me," shouted Dickon, and made a threatening movement with the knife, which he now drew.

"Touch her!" cried the boy, "and I will shoot thee with thine own pistol. The silver bullet will, mayhap, set free thy black soul."

At that same moment Guavas appeared from his room, where he had been, after the manner of miners, changing clothes on leaving work.

The moment Dickon saw him, he uttered a cry of rage, and rushed forward brandishing his knife. The boy, ignorant how to use a pistol, in vain endeavoured to discharge it. The pistol was, in fact, not cocked. Dickon grasped his arm and would have wrenched the weapon from him had not Guavas intervened and, taking the pistol from the boy's hand, cocked it and presented it at the head of Rawle.

"Quick," called Eldad, "bring cords that I may bind him; he is beyond his senses and wilt do mischief with his knife."

"There are the pack-horse ropes in the saddle room," said the boy.

" Bring them me."

When the lad had returned with the cords, then Eldad said to Dickon, " Put down thy knife."

The angry, baffled man reluctantly obeyed. He dared not offer further resistance with the pistol mouth gaping in his face.

" Lemonday," said Guavas, " hast thou courage to hold the pistol to his head whilst I bind him ? Pull the trigger only if he attempts to break away. At the least motion, the smallest resistance, press with thy forefinger there."

" I will do it," said the girl.

" I pray thee," urged Mistress Ford, " do not shed his blood here. I have enough to bear without that——" She cut her sentence short.

" Fear not," answered Eldad, " if blood is shed, it will be his doing. I will bind him fast, and cast him forth at the door."

Rawle was quaking with fear. Truculent he was, and cowardly withal.

The girl held the pistol as directed, not without tremor, but with resolve to fulfil exactly what she was bidden do by Eldad. He rapidly fastened Rawle's hands behind his back, so fast that it would not be possible for him to disengage himself.

"I pray you," he pleaded, "send me not out into the night.   I saw the wolf go by not an hour agone, and if he came on me now, and my hands thus tied——"

"Then use thy legs. I warrant they are nimble enough," said Eldad.

Then taking Rawle by the shoulders, and holding the end of the rope, he led him forth beyond the enclosing walls of the farm, and sent him adrift on the moor.

Night had settled in dark as Erebus, with clouds hanging low, and pouring forth torrents of rain, the darkness now and then relieved by gleams of lightning.

Then Eldad returned to the house, and seating himself on the bench, took up and examined the knife which Dickon had been forced to lay down on the table.

"The brach and the hound hunt together," he said with a bitter smile.

Dickon Rawle stood without, in the rain and lightning and explosions of thunder, shivering ; he leaned against the hedge outside the farm gate. In the darkness he knew not his way. At every moment he feared to be fallen on by the wolf. When the wind soughed among the coarse grass, or the water decanting from some eave splashed on a stone, he thought he heard the footfall of his

foe. The hillside sloped rapidly towards the river
How was he to cross the stream with bound
hands ? As the stones were slippery with wet,
should his feet give way, he would fall and break
a bone or dislocate a joint. An agony of terror
had come over him, completely dispelling his
manhood. He called, in the hopes that Isolt on
the hill opposite might hear, and come to his
assistance ; and yet he doubted whether she were
there, in the darkness and rain. Surely before
the blackness of night and storm fell she would
have made her way home.

In all his attempts against Guavas he had met
with discomfiture. This increased his rage and
hate, and he swore that should another occasion
offer he would not spare his enemy.

Yet now he had no thought as to means and
time of revenge ; he was concerned only with his
own safety.

He shrieked. He thought he saw two eyes
glare at him out of the darkness. It was but a
couple of tufts of cotton grass lighted by a flicker
of the retreating electric fire. Again he shrieked ;
he felt something at his neck under the ear. It
was but a wet bush of heather on the wall, swayed
by the wind against him.

He took three steps forward towards the river,
but retreated again towards the house, from

which a faint light issued, forming a halo in the vapour and rain. Within that circle of light there was some security. His cries would summon the Fords. They would not suffer him to be mangled and devoured by the wolf. Within the radius of that light he would be near human beings, even though such were ill-disposed towards him ; that were better than to be alone. If he got beyond the ray he might stray and lose himself in the bogs, and should he escape the wolf, yet might perish in the mire. To plunge into one of these terrible swamps with bound hands would be fatal. The one chance a man has in sinking is to extend his arms wide, and so obtain support from the moss and water-weed that lie on the surface. With tied wrists he would sink, and, on rising, never come to the surface, as the net-work of vegetation cast over the water would hold him down. Rawle shuddered and turned sick at the prospect. Then he heard steps at his side, started, and shrieked out.

"Be not afraid," said a voice. "It is I, Joan Ford."

"Let me into shelter. Hide me anywhere—in a linney, in a turf-stack—till day !" pleaded the wretched man.

"Nay," she answered ; "I will not do that, but I will release thee. Here, hold out th hands, that I may cut the knots that constrained them."

He extended his bound wrists, and with a knife she released him.

"There," she said, "take this and thy purse also, that thou didst leave on the table, as likewise thy pistol. I will have none of thy money, and with the weapon thou canst protect thyself from assault of ravenous beast. Go thy way—yonder it lies, whence the wind comes—keep it ever in thy face, and thou wilt not err. The clouds are breaking, and the crocks on the face of the moor will be thy guide. Come not this way again."

Dickon waited till she had departed, then he muttered, "In such a night I will not venture. I will even go to the blowing house where there is shelter as also warmth. I will tarry there till the door opens in the morning, and I will lie in wait, and will shoot him dead with the silver bullet!"

CHAPTER XXIII

AN EVIL EYE

NEXT morning Eldad made inquiries as to the direction in which lay Chaw Gully. He did not ask of Mistress Ford, though he told her with a smile that he should not rest content till he had discovered whence her husband had brought the spalls that lay among the heather, near the entrance to the house, and which he had tried at the christening of the kiln and had found rich in metal. But she seemed to divine his purpose and to be concerned about it.

Joan Ford took Guavas by the hand and led him forth out of the house, and seated herself on a stone where she might be overheard of none.

"Eldad," said she, with agitation in her voice and manner, "I must even now speak a word with thee, or ever thou proceedest further in this matter. Dost thou recall that night when first thou didst come to my door?"

"Very well indeed, mother."

"It was afore my good man was taken to his burial. I was troubled about laying him in the ground laden as he was with his sins till one had come and taken them off. Then thou didst enter at my door, and to thee was given the soul-cake, dipped in salt from off his breast, and with the eating thereof thou didst burden thyself with his transgressions."

"It is an idle fancy," said Eldad, with jest in his voice.

"It is no idle fancy, and thou hast no occasion to mock," retorted Joan Ford; "of that thou mayst judge for thyself, for on thee has fallen the consequence of his sin."

"What consequence ? "

"What has been on thee ever since that night save the enmity of Dickon Rawle ? Wherefore has that come ?"

"That is easily answered. I quarrelled with him at Crockern Stannary Hall, and for that reason and through envy at my fancied success, and the gall of malice that lies in the grounds of his mean heart, he stirred up a false charge against me of having defrauded the Queen, and obtained my punishment by the overbearing might of the bailiff, Rodda, and then——"

"Aye, and then—thou didst set thy wolf at his throat."

"I appealed to the judgment of God against the lawless judgment of men."

"Twice has Dickon Rawle sought thy life, and twice hast thou been delivered. But let me tell thee that deep under all fancied wrongs, such as revenge stirred by a brawl and envy of thy success, lies a real wrong. I must e'en speak the truth to thee ; as thou hast stepped in ankle deep, thou must go further over knee and know all. Dickon *must* follow thee, and seek thy life, not for that he covets thy tin but for that his brother Roger was killed and his blood is unavenged."

"I had naught to do therewith."

"Nay, that is certain, but my man Elias had. And on thee has come the guilt, for that thou didst eat the soul-cake and carry away his sin."

Eldad was startled and shocked.

"Mother Joan," he said in a low tone, "every man must bear his own burden. As a man soweth even so must he reap."

"If thou wilt quote Scripture I can do the same. One doth sow and another doth reap. My man did that which was against God's law and took the life of Roger Rawle, lest he should come to know whence he got the spalls of pure tin."

"Then it was in the Roman mine," exclaimed Eldad exultantly.

"I know nothing further—save only that he was the occasion of Rawle's death. That weighed heavily on his soul, and the consciousness of sin I verily believe was the cause of his sickness and death. After having committed that evil deed he never held up his head ; and to me alone he spake of it, and he revealed what he had done only when Death knocked at the door. Then he said that he could never enter into God's grace and rest in his grave, but must walk, unless his sin were taken away. And I, knowing that, sought to lay it on another. By heaven's favour thou wast sent to my door at my desire, and thou didst freely take on thee the sin and didst eat the cake. Therefore is it that the wrath of Rawle is kindled and flameth against thee. He knoweth not that his brother was foully done away with, but his brother's blood in him rebels and rises against and pursues the man on whom the guilt of that death lieth."

Eldad had a mind in advance of his time ; he regarded the practice of sin-eating, then almost fallen in desuetude, as a monstrous superstition, but he was startled at the coincidence of the implacable hostility of Rawle following him, dogging his every step almost from the moment when, according to the popular idea, the guilt of the murder had been transferred to him from the dead man.

"Now," said Joan Ford, "I beseech thee—follow my advice. I cannot forbid thee to seek the hidden lode in the haunted mine; thou must do so if thou art so disposed, but beware lest evil come on thee there. The sin there done is not extinguished, and its consequences may light on thee even at the place where the crime was committed."

"Mother," said Guavas, "thou knowest little of the Scriptures and nothing of the Christian religion, but clingest strangely to Popery, if thou holdest that sin can be carried from one to another, as I said once afore to Lemonday, by the eating of a cake dipped in salt. There is but One on whom sin can be laid, and who can bear the transgressions of man. Turn to Him and ask Him to bear the trespass of thy dead man, and I will join with thee and Lemonday, and it is written —Where two or three are united together as touching anything they shall ask, it shall be given them. All else is foolishness and fleshly ignorance, and against God's law and the Christian religion. I am sorry now that *I* did such a thing on the eve of Elias Ford's burial. Not that I apprehend the consequences, God forbid ! But that I cockered thee up in a wanton and heathenish superstition. Now, fare thee well for the day. Thou shalt have my hearty prayers for Elias. As to the pixie lode,

I feel that in me which urgeth me on towards it, and at all risks I must seek till I find it. Strive not therefore to dissuade me—for it availeth not."

Then Eldad moved in the direction of the blowing house. It was his intention to go there and look whether the tin were sufficiently cooled to be turned out of the mould, and whether he should fire the kiln anew.

He stood still, after having gone some distance, hesitating. He was within sight of the blowing house. Within was Dickon Rawle, holding the pistol. Rawle peered through the small window, and saw the Cornishman. He observed him approach, then halt, bite his thumb, and fall into a musing fit.

At that moment a hare ran athwart the path in front of Eldad.

Man is inconsistent. It was perhaps not strange that at such a period Guavas should be guilty of the inconsistency of arguing against superstition, and yet yield himself to it. He was a religious man, and because of that he saw that the superstition of Joan Ford was against the Christian faith, whereas that of attending a warning was not so of necessity—nay, it might be in accordance with religion to obey a warning, for were not tokens sent from above ? Now the crossing of his path by a hare when leaving the house the first thing in the morning is notoriously a warning to turn back. Guavas at once obeyed. He did not look upon his so doing as a superstitious act, but as a recognition of the hand of God. He turned aside at right angles with altered purpose. At the same moment, with an oath, Rawle lowered his pistol, and withdrew from the window. Eldad for the nonce had escaped him. The hare had delivered the Cornishman from the silver bullet.

Guavas now purposed to go direct to the head of the Webburn, and examine the Roman mine in Chaw Gully. He had inquired of Roger Gale where it was, and had received directions, by means of which he believed it would not be possible for him to miss it.

But it would little avail him to find old workings, shafts, and heaps of refuse, unless he could also descend into the bowels of the earth and discover the lode itself where it had been worked by Elias Ford. For this purpose he needed a stout cord. He had learned from the old hind that there were ruins near the stream head, where he could probably obtain a beam to which to fasten the cord.

Without saying anything about his intention to Joan Ford, he went into an outhouse where implements and lumber were kept, and thence took a cord, very strong and new, about twenty yards in length.

He was not afraid of goblins. He was too pious a man for that. He held that he had in him sufficient Christian faith to rout them, should they oppose his descent into their stronghold. As to the danger of going down a shaft, of that he had no dread. He had been a miner all his days, sometimes working surface tin, but sometimes engaged in mining underground.

He sought what was more difficult to procure —some clay; but this also he found at last with the assistance of the boy; and finally he took with him a piece of taper and flint and steel; then, as he was about to sally forth, he saw the anxious face of Lemonday. She had come forth to milk the cow, and she stood doubtful, with pale face, looking at him.

He went up to her, burdened with the coil of rope.

" Whither art' going ?" she asked.

" If you wilt know, I will answer; but I had as lief thou didst not ask."

" I wish to know. But, indeed, I suspect, for I see my mother is ill at ease. Look you, Eldad, there is a mystery. My father found a lode, like which there is none other, and there was at the time much talk concerning it, and he was watched.

They said he found the ore in Chaw Gully, where is the old Roman mine, but whether it was there or elsewhere I know not. One thing I do know —that Dickon Rawle's brother, who went there seeking it, met his death in the Roman mine. I pray thee do not venture thy life therein."

Guavas threw down the rope at her feet, and extended his arms, and took the girl's hands.

"Lemonday," said he, earnestly, and he fixed his eyes searchingly on hers, "it must be that I go. I am a poor man. Of what I had I have been robbed. My hand I shall never be able to use as afore. I go to find the pixie lode, and lay my claim to it, and then I shall be a rich man, and have a right to come here, and ask thee to be mine own."

The girl coloured, her eyes filled, and she fell on his breast. He clasped her to his heart.

"There is no need for thee to search for the Keenly Lode," she whispered. "My mother knows where it is. My father wrote in a book where it lies and how it is to be reached; but he bade her swear never to reveal it till one came; it was to be my dower."

"Lemonday," answered Guavas, "we men value not a free gift, but what we win for ourselves. I will not have the knowledge of the lode and access to it as a gift, even though brought by thee. I will have it because I have found it for myself, and I can bring it to thee. Dost understand ? I have pride. I esteem thee so highly, and in thyself I think thee so surpassingly precious, that I cannot receive from thee thyself and this wealth beside. If thou givest me thyself, I must have somewhat to give thee on my part and in return."

Suddenly Lemonday disengaged herself from his arms with a cry. On the other side of the wall, seated on her horse, was Isolt Rodda, with her mouth set, her eyes glaring, and her dark brows knitted.

Isolt said not a word, but turned the head of her horse and rode away.

"Come," said Guavas, "I go, and I trust to return with the secret open to me."

"Oh, Eldad ! Eldad ! if thou do but come back alive !"

"Fear nothing."

"I do fear. She who has even now gazed on us has the evil eye, and she looked at thee in such a manner as bodes only ill. She has ill-wished thee, and thou didst not cross thy thumbs."

"I fear her not," laughed Eldad, "for have I not one here to wish me well ; and a good wish from a generous heart will ever conquer one that is ill, as an upper wind ever masters that which is below."

CHAPTER XXIV

THE HAUNTED MINE

ELDAD gathered up the coil of rope, and, without looking whither Isolt had gone, he strode away in the direction of the Webburn Head.

The way was rough and wild, over moors, among rocks, down into valleys in which brawled foaming streams, among bogs where the cotton grass waved, and the surface seemed strewn with fluttering tufts of swan's down. He was occupied with his thoughts, and did not look behind him, otherwise he might have seen that he was followed stealthily, at a distance, by Dickon Rawle and Isolt, who took every opportunity afforded by the broken nature of the country to conceal themselves. They were both on foot. Isolt had left her horse at the blowing house.

The distance Eldad had to walk was not inconsiderable. He reached at length the high ground where stood the " King's Oven." This was a circular enclosure on the moor side, within which was a hut formerly inhabited by the royal smelter, and in the midst was a furnace in which the smelting took place. Formerly it had been customary for all tinners to deliver over to the Crown a certain percentage of the black tin found by them, and this black tin was then smelted at the " King's Oven." But this usage had been discontinued, and the much simpler arrangement had been come to of toll in money taken for all white tin produced. Originally one-thirteenth of all ore raised had to be delivered over by the miners at this royal oven. Such was the arrangement in 1288, but this was exchanged in 1305 to a fee of four shillings per hundredweight, and then the royal furnace ceased to be employed. Unhappily, some years ago, at the construction of two houses for miners hard by, the old royal blowing house was destroyed, and now nothing remains of it but a small heap of stones.

A strange appearance was presented by the valleys and lateral coombes at this point. Evidently the deposits of surface tin must at one time have been abundant, for the valley bottoms had been turned over and thrown up in rubble heaps ; every dip in the moors had been explored. It was as though giant plough-shares had been run in random fashion over the land, tearing deep trenches, throwing up huge heaps. In places the moor-face was pock-marked with the burrowing pits of costeeners; ruins of old mine buildings remained in the last stages of decay. What amount of tin was produced here in prehistoric times there are no data on which to found an opinion. The earliest information we have relative to this tin farm of the Crown dates from King John's reign. Then two-thirds of the tin produced came from these moors, and one-third only from Cornwall. In the course of the thirteenth century the production of Dartmoor dwindled; whereas that of Cornwall increased. In 1200 the annual produce of Dartmoor was but 120 tons of tin, whereas that of Cornwall had risen to 420 tons. In 1600 Cornwall produced 700 tons, and Devon but thirty.

This declension was due to the exhaustion of the deposits of surface tin, and to the scanty pursuit of stanniferous veins below the soil. Here and there parties of adventurers had combined to carry on mines underground, but the cutting into granite was laborious, and had not hitherto proved productive. These attempts had invariably resulted in disappointment and ruin.

Nevertheless there was always present an eagerness in the miners to combine, and in merchants to adventure money, induced by traditional tales of the enormous wealth in tin ore formerly produced on this granite desert. If tin was anciently found on the surface, that, it was agreed, proved that tin existed below the surface, and in all probability the further down the excavations went the richer and larger the veins would be found. Men considered at that period that metal grew in the rock like a tree. It had its trunk far down, probably quite out of reach, from which trunk extended branches, and from the branches twigs, and these twigs bore leaves or fruit. Such leaves or fruit were the surface tin, shed in the streamings. Below veins were to be found; the so-called veins were the ramifications of the tin tree. The miner had but to find and follow a living twig to reach a branch, and a branch of solid tin would furnish him with untold wealth. Failure had been due to adventurers finding and pursuing broken twigs, and so failing to reach the branches from which they had started

Eldad had not much difficulty in finding the special gully he sought by the directions given him. It lay between a tor rising to a crown, a great cairn, and a sweep or shoulder of moor marked by lines of upright stones, a relic of hoar antiquity, indicating the place of memorial of dead warriors.

He found the gully to be a very singular place, indeed. It was manifestly cut down in the hillside by the hands of men, hewn out of the solid rock to a depth of some forty feet. The workers had endeavoured, so long as possible, to carry on operations in daylight, but also it was apparent, on close observation, that, unable to slash deeper into the rock, and still urged on by greed for metal, they had sunk wells at the bottom of this cleft—shafts by which they might descend to the main trunk, or, at least, the great branches of the tin tree, whose roots were in the heart of the earth.

These shafts were carefully built about in a manner very unusual in the Middle Ages. Popular tradition told of their being the mining works of the Romans, but no evidence of any working of mines in Roman times had been found there. Would-be learned men talked of Phœnicians, with just as little evidence. The vulgar were quite as near the truth when they said " they reckoned the pixies had a done it."

The method employed in cleaving the rocks was remarkable. No gads and wedges had been employed, no sign of iron tool was visible, and the saying was that the hewing had been done by grooves painfully worked in the stone, then these filled with lime, upon which water was poured, when the sudden expansion of the lime rent the rocks asunder.

That such a method was pursued at one time is probable, otherwise it would be difficult to account for the tradition.

Guavas ascended the ravine, between beetling crags and steep slopes of fine rubble, that was now densely overgrown with heather, disturbing, as he advanced, numerous birds, rock-pigeons, ravens, ring-ouzels. It was warm in this gorge, the rocks of which cut off all winds, and, by the winding of the course, made loops which the sun filled with heat, and where bumble-bees and moths revelled and where also adders basked. Some of these latter, lying on the warm shale, raised their heads, looked at the intruder, and were too inert in their enjoyment to writhe away.

Guavas passed two holes like funnels, but without an opening below. He knew that they were shafts which had fallen in and were choked. There was a mighty crag, from the hedge of which started a raven, and, where the ravine contracted to a narrow black gate, he saw an open well yawning at his feet. He looked down it and could see no bottom. He dropped a stone, that bounded from side to side, but made no splash in water or thud on hard bottom. He examined the stones on all sides of this pit-mouth, but could see no pieces rich in metal, only black with hornblende and micaceous iron, or white with spar. He raised the tufts of heather to see whether Elias Ford had secreted anywhere deposits of ore. He could find none. Yet this was almost certainly the place where Roger Rawle had descended and had lost his life. This was the way to the Pixie Lode, for it was to prevent the discovery of this lode that Elias had cut the cord by which Rawle was suspended, and had precipitated him to the bottom.

How had Ford descended ?

There were no projecting stones ; no holes for feet and fingers in the walled sides of the shaft by which a hardy climber might descend or ascend. He must have entered by some other opening known only to himself. Should he, Eldad, search for this ? It was probably some second open shaft, the mouth concealed by an overgrowth of heather or gorse. If so, he would have to descend that in the same way as he purposed going down this well. It mattered not whether he found the other. The fact that here was that where Rawle was killed by Elias Ford sufficed to show that by this orifice, and in this way, the treasure was to be reached.

Eldad was now satisfied that he must descend at this point. He had not found an oak beam among the ruins that would suit his purpose, but he had provided himself with what would serve his object equally well, a stout crowbar.

This he now rammed into the soil of the side of the gully near the pit-mouth. He did more than that; he heaped masses of rock about it so that the bar was made absolutely firm in an upright position, and would stand a strain such as would be caused by his weight suspended from it. It would do more than that; it would not yield to a jerk.

Well satisfied that the bar was secure, he looped the cord firmly round it and proceeded, seated in the glowing sun, to make knots in the cord at intervals of two feet, and thrust a tough piece of stick here and there athwart each knot, thus making a ladder with hold for hands and feet.

Guavas was not alarmed at the prospect before him. As a boy he had been over cliffs on the Cornish coast, and he had been down mines in the tin and copper districts. To be underground presented no terrors to his mind. He did not disbelieve in pixies and underground spirits, but he was confident that they could not hurt a man who believed in God. But there was risk undoubtedly; the stones built about the shaft were not set in mortar, and on being touched might be dislodged. The cord might grate on a sharp

HE SWUNG HIMSELF OVER, AND WENT DOWN THE IMPROVISED ROPE LADDER,

quartz edge and be cut through. But Guavas made provision against both contingencies by fastening together a faggot of heather, over which he carried his rope so that it should hang clear of the stone-work. The raven was perched above on the rock screaming ; an adder, coiled on a flat stone, fixed its glittering eyes on the man preparing to plunge into darkness, and hissed. Eldad kneaded the clay he had brought with him, and affixed the lump to his cap, passing it under the strap, and then into the clay he thrust the end of a taper, unlighted. He had need to economise his light ; he would not require artificial illumination till he had reached the bottom and was in an adit.

He seated himself on the brink, looked up to the blue sky and said : " Joseph to the tinner's aid, and with the good wishes of Lemonday."

Then he swung himself over, and went down the improvised rope ladder.

His eyes were now attentively fixed on the sides. He was speedily below where the walling of the shaft began, and was descending through a well cut in the solid rock. Ferns and moss clustered in every cranny, waving with the air that descended with him. The sides glistened with moisture or with spar. A great snail was there ; it had drawn a shining track on the rock.

Cobwebs had been spun across the angles. In one case Guavas passed through one, and saw a huge spider dart away and disappear in a hole, as he rent the meshes of the net.

Then he perceived an opening at the side. Here it was that Elias had stood and had cut the cord by which Rawle was suspended. He went past it—a descent of several yards—and then his feet rested on a soft mass of peat. He was at the bottom. The depth was not so considerable as he had anticipated, or rather as had been represented. He looked up, and saw the blue sky, indigo blue, with the pale moon like a ghost shining in it.

Then he stepped aside into a passage that went into the heart of the mountain.

There he drew forth his tinder and flint and steel, and struck sparks that kindled the tinder. He blew it to produce a flame by which to light his taper. As he blew his eyes rested on the pale bluish patch of light at the bottom of the well, the reflection from the sky above, and in this hung the cord, each knot showing distinctly, as though illuminated by phosphorous, owing to the falling light that rested on it. All at once, to his surprise, he saw the entire rope come down, and fall as a coil to the bottom. He had not time to be alarmed, only surprised, when the fall of the rope was followed by a crash of stones. They came down in rapid succession, as though the whole walling of the mouth of the shaft were giving way.

He did not dare to venture from under cover and look up, lest one of these blocks should strike him. His breath failed. The flame he was kindling expired; only the glowing tinder remained in his hand. He looked now in real dismay. By what means could he reascend? How was it that the casing of stones was precipitated down the shaft? Was the whole shelf of rubble into which he had driven the crowbar moving downwards and pouring in?

The atmosphere was charged with dust, a fog of fine powder, in which nothing could be clearly distinguished. The means of seeing anything became rapidly less, and then ceased altogether. He was in darkness—absolute it would have been but for the tiny red spark in his hand.

He was buried alive five fathoms underground.

CHAPTER XXV

IN DARKNESS

LEMONDAY sat in the sun spinning, and, as she spun, she sang :

> He took his horse all by the head,
> And swift away did ride ;
> She gathered up her skirts and ran
> All by his stirrup side.
> And when she to a river came,
> She bent her breast and swam ;
> And when she was on the green grass,
> Then swift afoot she ran.
> He never was a courteous knight,
> To bid her mount and ride,
> And she was such a simple maid
> She bid him not abide.

She ceased spinning and singing as she sat looking dreamily before her. She was not thinking of her spinning nor of the ballad. She was following Guavas in thought, as he trudged along over hill and down dale. Her heart was heavy with care, but, whether heavy or light, she must sing. It is so with the birds of the air ; it is so with the natural man and woman—to sing is a necessity.

> " Now stay, the night is falling dark,
>   And weary thou must be."
> " I will not stay by night or day,
>   But run 'long side of thee."
> And when they came to London town,
>   He from her off did fling ;
> She hasted to the king's palace
>   And knocked at the ring.

" That, Guavas would never have done. Nay, he was not going to London, but to seek the Pixie Lode." And, as he went, her mind ran alongside of him. And now he was come to Chaw Gully. She had never been there. She figured it in her mind other than it really was.

All at once there came upon her an overwhelming feeling of horror, freezing her marrow, laming her fingers, stiffening her tongue. It was like the roll of a cold wave enveloping her, depriving her for the moment of breath, even of sight. It passed, and left her shivering and gasping, and impressed with the sense of disaster having overtaken her friend, Eldad Guavas. The sun had lost its light and heat for her ; she dropped her work, unable to pursue it, and staggered into the house.

" Oh, mother, mother ! " she said, breathless, " something has happened ! "

"What—is the cow took bad ?"

"No—mother—he—Eldad."

"What of him ?"

"I am sure some'ut be wrong, I'm that terrified. I feel it—I know it."

"Where is he ?"

"I reckon he be gone to Chaw Gully."

"To Chaw Gully ?" repeated the widow, her face cold and hard.

"Yes, mother; he were that bent on finding the Pixie Lode, that nothing would hold him. He took a cord and a bar, and now I'm sure something has befallen him."

"If he will risk goin' where he didn't ought——"

"Oh, mother ! what is to be done ? I'm sure he is in danger. It came upon me as if I heard him a calling to me ; and I'm sure if I don't help, he'll never live."

"He must take the consequence of his own folly. I reckon he's gone down that same place where Roger Rawle met his death. It's fool-hardiness."

"Mother—I *must* help him ; and there's only one way. Let me see the pages you cut out of father's book. I'm sure that therein are directions about the old Roman mine."

"My child," said Joan Ford, "in that mine is

the treasure that will form some day your dower.
I have sworn to your father that none shall have
the secret how to lift it but he who takes you to
wife."

"Then you may e'en tell me," said the girl, in
her distress the sweat running off her pale brow.
"Mother, if Eldad and me weren't ordained to
be one flesh, however would it happen that I feel
this ill come on him just the same as if it had
come on myself?"

"Lor' bless ye," answered the widow, "I felt a
cold creep all down my backbone, just as though
a toad were there, when you come in frightening
of me. I thought it was the cow had milk fever.
That don't show we're one flesh."

"No, mother, because the cow is lusty and
well. But I'm, as it were, promised to Eldad,
and I won't never take anyone else for very sure,
and he said the same to me."

"Oh, promises and all that," said the mother,
contemptuously. "I don't hold by they. Let
them be fast made wi' ring and book, and then
it's other games altogether."

"Mother, let me see the cut-out pages."

"I may let you see them, child," said Joan
Ford, after consideration, "if you'll promise to
me that you'll tell Eldad nought till he's made
you his own fast, as I said."

"But I may use for his assistance what I find ?"

"If ill-luck have befallen him, and you can help, you may do so. But tell nothing before the time."

After much persuasion the old woman was induced to produce the leaves that she had extracted from the pigskin bound book. Lemonday spread them on the table and considered them attentively.

"Mother," she said, "may Roger Gale and the boy come with me ?"

"No," answered the widow; "if any one goes, it shall be I. After all, if anything have happed to Guavas we must do what us can for him. I've a kind of liking for the man myself."

Lemonday folded the parchment sheets, and put them in her bosom, and the two women were speedily on their way to Chaw Gully.

When Eldad was buried in darkness, and realised that the means whereby he had entered the haunted mine were no more available for exit, he remained for a moment considering what he must do.

It was possible for him, when the fall of earth and stones came to an end, to set to work and remove them; the mass that had fallen in could hardly be so great that by patience he could not clear it away below so as to again reach light. But what would this avail him ? The rope by which he had descended was cast down, and it would not be possible for him to climb the shaft without its assistance.

Whether the collapse of the sides was due to accident, or whether some enemy had wilfully dislodged the stones was uncertain, but the latter seemed most probable. The cord would not of its own accord have disengaged itself from the bar and slipped down. Had the bar given way it would have come down together with the line.

He blew the tinder to a flame, and kindled the taper. He could look about him. Now he saw the shaped stones mingled with rubble that choked the mouth of the adit in which he stood. The gallery he was in was small, narrow, and only sufficiently high to admit of his standing upright for a few yards in from the opening.

The light he had in his cap could not last him. for more than a couple of hours, and then he would be indeed in utter darkness. What he must do during the time whilst light was at his command was to explore the ancient mine, and discover whether there were not some other means of exit than the gallery leading to the shaft. Accordingly he stooped, and slowly, cautiously, proceeded along the passage.

He had been ill-wished, and the ill-luck had come on him ; but he had also been well-wished, and he was sanguine that escape was before him.

As he passed along, there were places where water stood on the floor, and he was forced to wade in slime. The walls glittered with tears, oozing out of faults in the strata.

He was observant as he went along. The tunnel was cut in elvan, a fine, white-grained formation that is usually found in connection with mineral veins, and here and there was a run of porphyritic granite, reddened by heat, as the molten metal was driven through the rents of the superincumbent rocks, riving, altering them in its passage. Eldad knew nothing of geology, which was a science not even in its infancy at that date, for it was not even supposed to exist ; but he had a shrewd, experimental knowledge of the tokens of metal. He scooped up some of the flockan—the clay—and saw in it tokens of the presence of tin. But he had not time to waste in search after metal ; he must find a mode of escape from his underground prison.

Now and then he passed lateral passages. Some seemed to ascend, none descended. He was therefore on the lowest level.

He hesitated for a moment whether to take one of these galleries that gave promise of leading to a higher stage, but on further consideration deemed it advisable first to explore to its extremity that in which he was.

All at once he emerged into a sort of hall, a circular chamber, in which, to his relief, he was able to stand upright. As he could touch the roof that was beaded with waterdrops, he knew he was not under a choked shaft.

From this chamber six tunnels branched in different directions. He turned to examine each opening and determine which he should pursue, and then found that he had lost his bearings, and could not recall by which he had entered. He was angry with himself for his lack of consideration in not having marked the opening of the tunnel by which he had obtained access to the hall. He examined the floor for his traces, but here there was little mud, and every opening resembled another save one, and that one had a piece of white spar on the ground at the entrance.

This was placed there for a purpose; and to discover that purpose Eldad resolved to follow that gallery. Again he stooped and went forward. He was obliged to use caution lest he should strike his head against a projecting portion of the roof, and lest the drops of moisture should extinguish his candle.

Presently he saw before him in the slime at the

bottom, the print of a man's foot, as fresh as his own newly-made. None had been in there since Elias Ford. This must have been made by him, and by this way he had either gone to the vein of metal or found his way back.

A little further, and by the faint light of his taper Eldad saw a miner's pick and a heap of "spalls." He went down on his knees eagerly and examined the pieces. They were nearly pure tin. In the rock the same indications, and here the gallery stopped; the vein had never been worked out, but abandoned where richest. In his joy at having discovered the secret, Eldad gave a shout, and at that moment the candle fell out of its clay holder and was extinguished in a pool of water at his feet.

He seated himself on the broken pieces of ore, groped for the candle, and endeavoured in vain to relight it. The wick was too wet to be ignited.

There was no help for it; in the dark he must feel his way back to the hall from which the passage radiated. But when there—how proceed? He put the bit of candle—it was but an inch—in his bosom, in the hope that the warmth of his body might dry the wick.

After a while he was back in the chamber. He could feel that the walls fell back to right and left, but in which direction he should proceed he knew not. He cast himself on the floor and waited for his candle end to be dried. All was still, save that he could hear the monotonous drip of water far off, like the ticking of a death-watch. Time passed, but how he could not judge in rayless darkness ; time was articulated only by the dropping of the water. He counted the drops—a thousand—and then would try to kindle his candle end. Alas ! the dampness of the atmosphere did not favour the process. Again the wick refused to flame. His tinder was nigh expended. It would last him but for one more trial. He must again wait for a thousand drops to fall before he made his final effort.

And when the thousand had been counted he was fearful, and counted five hundred more, and then struck sparks and ignited the last remaining fragment of tinder. It glowed, the sparks ran, he blew, applied the candle-wick. In vain ; he blew more strongly, and the sparks went out. His tinder was exhausted. He was doomed to darkness. He threw down the taper-end in despair.

How time passed he could not tell. He ceased counting the fall of water-drops. Only at long intervals, in great horror and craving for light, he struck sparks with his flint, and was momentarily relieved by the sight of the flash ; then sank back again against the rock.

For long his mind worked, and then ceased to exert itself. It stopped like an unwound clock, and yet after a while became active again. Roused once more, he endeavoured to crawl into one of the galleries. He pursued it for some way, came to an abrupt termination and retraced his steps; then became confused. He thought he had branched off in the darkness into a lateral passage, and lost his direction as wholly as one who wanders in a fog.

CHAPTER XXVI

IN FOXTOR MIRE

ISOLT RODDA and Dickon Rawle were returning from Chaw Gully. A savage triumph fired the handsome features of the girl, but the man was pallid and shaken.

"By heaven!" said Isolt, "I'd like to go straight up to that wench, Lemonday, and tell her that her lover is buried alive, and that he never will come up, never stand by her in Widecombe Church; nay, not even to be laid in Christian earth."

"As to his coming up, I'm not sure that he mayn't," answered Dickon. "But alive he never will. Was not my brother brought from below and laid on the shale heap?"

"He was not buried with stones heaped over him, Dickon. I defy the spirits to remove all that we have cast in to choke the shaft and smother the fool who descended it. He is there till the crack of doom. And I am glad. I am glad. He

has mocked and slighted me. None shall do that and come off scatheless; so beware thyself, Dickon."

"Isolt," said the young man, "be guided by my council. Let us not return the same way, but make a round by Sherill and the Walla Brook; it would be ill for both of us were we called in question for this day's work."

"Who is to call us in question?" scoffed the girl. "Who saw what was done? Who can say that we did it with evil purpose? that we were not as wanton boys and girls who throw stones into any holes they find to sound the depths? Who can declare against us that we knew a quick man was below? Nay; I fear not; but as to the way by Sherill, I doubt not it is no longer than by Bellever as we came; therefore have with you, Dickon."

Brutal and coarse as Rawle was, he was not so callous as to retain his usual spirits. The thought that he had done a man to death, though that man was one against whom he bore a grudge, weighed on him. Not that he felt compunction for his act, but that his base heart quailed at the consequences to himself, should it be known that he had killed Guavas, and should he be called to account for it.

The day was already in decline, and the distance to be made was great. Not only had they to go to the Swancombe blowing house for the horse of Isolt, but thence the way over the waste was one of many miles, and that through a peculiarly difficult portion of the moor to traverse, as destitute of prominent landmarks, and as being in proximity to a tract of extensive bog, of unfathomed depth and of treacherous surface, over which at night danced the will-o'-the wisp, and into which, when a horse plunged, if he came out again, it would be with phosphorescent gleams flickering along his wet hide.

The sun had set by the time they reached the River Dart at Hexworthy, near which the Strane that flows from Swancombe enters the Dart. As they approached a spot where was a tenement taken out of the moor, of ancient tenure, some one shouted to them. Rawle was alarmed, and would have run, but Isolt dissuaded him. "Fool!" she said; "put a bold face on't, and answer him boldly."

A man came up.

"Who be you ?" he asked.

"We are after some strayed sheep," answered Isolt. "Hast seen any marked with a cross and G ?"

The man shook his head. He did not know whom he was addressing, belonging as he did to another quarter of the moor.

“ How many ? ” he asked.

“ A score,” answered Isolt, promptly.

“ And they belong to you ? ”

“ To one named Gorman—at Brent.”

“ I’ll bear’t in mind if I sees ’em. Hast heard
the tidings ? ”

“ No ; what tidings ? ”

“ The Warden of the Stannaries is down at
Lydford, and has ordered the arrest of Rodda, the
bargmaster. Folk say it is a wonder he has been
allowed a free hand so long. He was a mighty
rogue, by all accounts. Do you know him ? ”

“ I know of him,” answered Rawle, to cover the
dismay and confusion of his companion.

“ Well,” said the moor-man, “ once he be fast
in Lydford Castle, I reckon he may as well say
good-bye to the world. There they hang and
draw, and sit in judgment after, as all the world
knows. I wish you good den, my master and
mistress. You have a longish walk to Brent afore
you.”

In silence and concern both made their way up
the Swancombe Brook to the blowing house,
there to discover, to their further discomfiture,
that Isolt’s horse had broken his bridle, and was
gone, and probably had returned to his home, for
he was out of sight.

Although the girl was tired, she had no alternative but to walk the rest of the way. Neither she nor Rawle was in humour for speech.

"It must be," she said shortly. "Lead on and waste no time."

As they ascended the flank of moor on the south side of the stream, they obtained a view of the house occupied by the Fords. No light burned in it ; no smoke issued from the chimney. They heard the lowing of the cow, impatient to be milked, angry at delay. The day had been fine and hot, but with set of sun a fog began to form over the hilltops and roll down the sides. It came up from the sea with the tide, and would probably last till turn of tide and then disperse. Such a phenomenon occurs occasionally, and when it does occur, and overtakes travellers on the moor, it is liable to throw them out of their course.

"This is desperate !" exclaimed Rawle, looking at the curtain of vapour descending towards them. "What is to be done ? There is no house near save that in Swancombe."

"I will die rather than shelter there," said Isolt.

"We may return to the blowing house," suggested Rawle.

"Push on ; if we lose our way we must find it again. The wind is from the south. We have but to keep our faces to it."

"In the fog we can follow no marks—not even feel the wind."

"We must set our faces boldly. Go on."

Next moment they were in fog, dense, palpable, charged with a heavy earthy savour.

"It has a rank smell," said the girl.

"It is rank with the corruption of Foxtor Mire, and, by heaven, unless we keep a right direction we shall be into it."

"My feet went into water even now."

"If we once get in," said Dickon, "not all the desire in one's heart to keep a right direction will help us to it. You will tie yourself up in a letter S; you will go round like a top; and in and out as in a maze; leaping from one bit of rush to another; now here, now there; and whether you face north, south, east or west there is nothing to tell; and whether you are going in deeper or getting near the margin you have no means of judging. A hundred chances to one, but when you are nigh dry ground you miss it and get into deep water. What is that?"

"I saw something—a sheep, maybe."

"It was not a sheep. 'Fore heaven, the mist is waxing thicker, and the dusk is falling deeper. Here is red fen." Then suddenly he uttered a cry and sprang on one side.

"The wolf! I swear he is tracking us!"

Rawle gasped. "I heard his snarl—I saw his teeth."

"If he come—shoot him!"

"I need no command to do that."

"It was but a sheep thou didst see. In vapour everything looks greater than it is, in truth."

"A sheep!" Then ensued a rush, and the grey beast would have fastened on him had not Rawle darted forward and turned to face it.

Isolt sprang aside.

The wolf indeed was there, but he did not seem to regard Isolt, certainly did not venture to molest her. He ran round and made sallies to fall upon Dickon, now disappearing in the fog, then leaping out of it from another direction, and if he found Rawle on the alert and facing him, ready to slink back and bury himself in the coils of vapour.

"By my soul!" said Dickon between his teeth, "since we've rid us of the Cornishman who sucked to him all the profits of our moors, his familiar was bound to go after him to the bottomless abyss whence he sprang. Thither I'll speed him when the chance comes." And planting himself on a tuft of grass, he spanned the cock of his pistol.

"'Fore heaven!"

In panic a bullock rushed by bellowing, close to Dickon and Isolt, and plunged into the morass. They saw it struggle to escape whence it had floundered. With violent effort it strove to heave itself on to solid soil, then in a paroxysm of terror take another step and go into mire and water again, plunge about, snort, bellow, churn the peaty water, tear the moss with its hoofs, and go under, and vanish from their sight with a suddenness that sent their blood to their hearts.

Neither spoke. Each knew full well that the poor brute had been scared by the wolf, and had fled from it to the marsh into which it had sunk, never to reappear. Bubbles were rising ; a tossing of the surface alone indicated where it had gone down.

Dickon recoiled. The sight of the death of the bullock before his eyes within a few paces was enough to scare him. Yet, whither was he to turn ? He was afraid of the firm land on which raced his deadly enemy, the wolf. He was afraid of the morass, hungry to swallow him. In the coils of vapour that circled about him, now lifting for a moment, then settling more dense than before, he was wholly unable to distinguish where was moor and where marsh.

He turned, however, away from the place where the bullock had disappeared, in hopes of reaching firmer soil than that on which for the moment he stood. But next moment he was undeceived.

" I am in ! " shouted Rawle, plunging to his

knees. He struggled to extricate himself, and in the struggle dropped the pistol. For a moment only. As he struggled to his knees on a patch of rushes, he recovered his weapon, but at the same moment felt a rush, a plunge, the snuffle and blast of breath about him—the grey wolf had leaped out of the smokelike vapour, and was on him. Blinded with terror, regardless of everything save his own safety, and too frightened to consider how best to defend himself and repel his assailant, he pulled the trigger. Instantly there was a flash, followed by a report. Then a shrill cry. The silver bullet had missed the wolf, and had struck Isolt in the breast.

She fell, and was on her knees with extended arms.

"Dickon ! Help ! I am shot !"

With a curse, he replied : " Help thyself. I have my own work to keep off the wolf."

He was beating about him with the butt end of the pistol. He hammered at the snout of the brute with the iron shod weapon. The beast howled, fell off, and made another rush. Dickon sprang to his feet, stepped back, endeavoured to reload, but dared not allow the wolf to catch him off his guard, to get behind, or on one side of him. And the savage, wily animal seemed to understand that if he suffered Dickon to recharge the pistol it would be fatal to himself, and therefore frantically leaped, and tore with his fore paws, striking at Rawle's hands as he feverishly laboured with the weapon. Then he backed snarling, made a leap, and fastened with his teeth on Rawle's chest; the fangs met in his jerkin, and bit into flesh as well. Rawle had no other means of escape than to throw himself on the ground and roll, battling with the wolf among moss and rushes, in mire and water.

Isolt remained kneeling, with hands extended, in horror at her own condition and at the death struggle before her. If in this grapple Dickon succumbed, what chance of escape was there for herself—alone, wounded, the blood bubbling from her breast, in fog, night settling in, away from every track. She could see indistinctly the writhing forms ; they seemed to tangle themselves in vapour, as though it were cobweb that they coiled around them as they strove. It was like a great cocoon of fine tissue with moving objects inside that screamed and snarled, that cursed and bayed. She was turning sick and faint. Unable to sustain herself on her knees, Isolt fell forward and rested on her palms, and saw the blood dribble from her, and form a pattern on the short grass. It fell on whortleberry leaves, and coloured them as though they were touched by an early frost; it stained crimson a tuft of cotton grass; and the fog, condensing on the blood-dyed tuft, diluted the red stain, and ran it in bloody tears down the stem that bent under the weight of moisture.

The vapour was whirling, spinning about her as though it were a teetotum of wool, and the spike on which it spun was in her breast, working its way in deeper, ever deeper, entering into her heart.

On her knees she crept forward towards the water, and scooped some up; she washed her breast, gathered moss, scrabbling it together with her hands, and held it to the wound to staunch the flow of blood. And then—it was the last thing her eyes saw, as they closed in a sick faint —the wolf was running triumphantly up and down beside a tract of peat water covered lightly with fibres of weed and patches of torn moss. It had its muzzle down, and was snuffing the ground; up and down it ran—up and down; then it stood still, pointing with its nose to the water. Out of the mire emerged a hand, clutching wildly in the air, the five fingers wide extended, then contracted, laying hold only of a tuft of moss, and then— sinking below the surface, with this piece of moss clenched so tight that it squeezed every drop of water out of it. That was the last ever seen of Dickon Rawle.

CHAPTER XXVII

INTO LIGHT

GUAVAS sat in darkness; he knew not where he was, whether in the central hall from which radiated the passages, or whether he had got into some other portion of the mine. In the dark, when once the mind has lost idea of direction, it can never recover it. Usually, with strange obliquity, it inverts the position of everything it last saw, and conceives the points of direction to be opposite to where they really are. He was sufficiently aware of this to know that it was hopeless for him to expect to find his way back to the place whence he had started. He might creep along where he found himself, on the chance of reaching an opening. The gallery he was in might bring him to the light of day. If it did not, his condition was past hope. Where he was, there he must rest till death relieved him, and there he must lie till the trumpet of the Archangel sounded to rouse the dead, and was heard even at that depth.

Guavas was a man of grave and religious mind, and he now calmly considered what lay before him, and from the abyss of discouragement raised his prayer to God, not to work a miracle for his release, but to strengthen him to endure what he deemed inevitable.

He had in his pouch some bread and meat, and this he now brought forth and proceeded to eat. It was the last meal he would ever take. He ate slowly; he was hungry. Thirsty he was not; the moisture around him, the dampness of the atmosphere in the mine prevented his feeling thirst.

Looking with open eyes before him into the nigritude of subterranean night, he had not the sense of being in absolute darkness. The eyes that have been in a sun-blaze, carry with them, as it were, an internal spring of light that feeds the eyes for long. A faint rosy halo seemed to surround him, in which he fancied that he could discern rocky protuberances and glittering metallic veins. If, however, he put forth his hand to touch what in imagination he saw, he became aware that the vision was unsubstantial.

And now he thought he heard the sound of little pickaxes upon the ore, and anon of small whispers passing along the gallery. He had heard of the pixies or gnomes who worked in disused mines, spirits of the earth that ruled over the veins of ore.

He had heard grave and sedate men tell that they had seen them underground, some had even been accosted by them. Guavas was not sufficiently in advance of his time to disbelieve in the supernatural. That there were such beings he thought possible enough; but he himself had never encountered one of them. Now he believed that he heard them. Possibly the drip of distant water to his excited fancy may have been construed as the strokes of elfish picks, and the sighing of a draught of air from some unknown opening, have been interpreted as fairy whispers.

And now Guavas began to think of Lemonday and at once a great ache woke in his heart. He could bear to lose his life, but to lose her—that was a prospect less endurable. Life was not, or had not been to him, so exceedingly precious. It had been one of daily toil, lightened whilst she lived, by the love of his mother, his only relative, the only one to whom his heart had clung. It had been without distinct purpose, his toil not directed to any goal. But of late, life had assumed to him a different complexion. It had been thrilled through with a new force; it had acquired a fresh significance; above all it had been given an aim. He loved Lemonday, and she had admitted that his love was not unrequited. She had rested on his heart; his arms had enfolded her that day for the first time, and for the first time his lips had touched her modest brow. There is a truth in the old fable of the Elixir of Life, that marvellous element which transmutes lead to silver, copper to gold. But the alchemists had not known where to search for it. They had peered after it in the wrong quarter, in the crucible over a coal fire. It had not entered their heads that the elixir gushed, a living, unfailing fountain, out of a pure woman's heart. To-day Guavas had tasted the Elixir of Life—Love—and his dull and sordid life had been transmuted to one most precious. Therefore it was that now the thought of Lemonday and of his loss became to him unbearable. There passed over his soul a wave of bitterness, and he felt himself a prey to agony that brought the sweat in streams from his brow, and made him clench his hands till the nails entered his palms.

He must make another effort to reach the light, to work himself out of his living tomb. He rose and went forward, groping with his hands, cautiously putting one foot before him ere he took a step, lest he should stumble on some down shaft, and fall to a lower level and be broken in that deeper depth, fathoms further from the light of day.

The moisture from the sides ran over his hands,

now water, then slime ; his feet trod on stones fallen from the roof, or sank in mud. Now a cold drop fell on his face and ran down it as though the very rock were melting and were weeping at his interment.

His feet stumbled over something.

He put down his hands and felt, and laid hold of a piece of what he supposed was wood, smooth, rounded. He measured it with his hands and found it was a pick handle. He groped further and was among broken spalls ; then his hand touched the rock.

He knew where he was ; he was again in that gallery which led to the pixie ore, the vein of pure tin, where Elias had resumed the work that had been abandoned centuries before by unknown miners, and had left there his tools. He had reached the very spot whence he had turned to retrace his steps. He had come again on the dead treasure, now valueless, and was as far as before from that living treasure, alone now of price—daylight—that would bring with it in its train the life of love and happiness.

Now he knew that if he turned, and went forwards touching the rock with his left hand, he must reach the central hall. If then he followed the wall, still touching, he must arrive at the entrance to another gallery, not yet explored.

There was some chance of life in this. Accordingly he turned back, and in process of time did reach what he believed was the chamber whence issued the radiating passages.

Still groping with his hand, he arrived at the opening to the next gallery, and entered that. He crept along—for how long he could not tell. He had lost all sense of time. The floor was unencumbered with stones, and the passage was comparatively dry.

Then his feet were trampling among things that clickered. He stooped and felt for that which he had disturbed. He laid hold of something like a pick-handle, but not of wood, not as heavy as wood. He felt along it; he raised it to his nose, and dropped it hastily. It was a bone. He considered a moment, then felt about once more, and his hands rested on some round object. He took it up, and groping, assured himself it was a human skull.

Some man—full of venture after the pixie treasure, the Keenly Lode—had entered the mine, lost his way, and perished there. And such would be his fate. Here he would moulder and go to dust, and his sole satisfaction was that here he would not fall a prey to the worm. Full of horror, Guavas turned once more and retraced his steps, and rested not till he had again reached the central chamber. When this took place he sank on the floor. His hope was failing—his strength was well nigh spent.

Lying thus, he tried to gather his thoughts, to recover his courage to prosecute his search ; but he could do neither, and out of weariness of brain and exhaustion of physical power he lapsed into a condition that was not sleep with dreams, and was not complete unconsciousness, but was stagnation of mind and nerve. In this condition he remained for long, looking before him into inky blackness, breathing, his heart beating slowly, cold sweat oozing from his pores and slowly trickling down, much as moisture oozed from the sides of the passages and dribbled down the sides. No thought moved in his mind ; he was conscious of no pain, of nothing, only of a tingling like the pricking of pins in his hands and feet, but that not painful, only disquieting.

Then he saw, but saw without emotion and without inquiry, a light travelling towards him. Who bore it, whether anyone bore it, he did not know or care to inquire. The light filled his eyes, poured through them into his heart that thirsted for light, and drank it in, and cared nothing in its overwhelming craving after light how it came and who gave it.

Then a cry of joy and pain. " Eldad ! " and in

another moment someone was by him, had clasped him. He felt warm breath play over his sweat-bathed face, a warm heart beat against his that was becoming slowly chilled, hot lips kiss his that were ice cold.

Now a sort of consciousness returned as to one waking out of a trance.

He rubbed his eyes, passed his hand over his brow, and suddenly his senses returned with a leap. His blood began to glow ; with a start his mind resumed activity, and springing up, he cried:

" Lemonday ! "

In a kiss he found life return, boiling through his veins like water bursting through a sluice.

" Lemonday ! I have found my treasure ! "

Did he mean the Keenly Lode, or the virgin ore in the girl's honest heart ? In his dazed condition he knew not what he meant.

Without, in the declining light of day, sat Joan Ford. The true entrance to the Roman mine had been discovered by her husband. Under a huge fallen slab of rock was a *cache*, a miners' hiding-place, with the end walled up. This wall, on being removed, revealed the opening to an adit. Whenever Elias entered the mine he removed this wall; whenever he left it he reconstructed the wall, so that the way into the old tin mine was once more effectually concealed.

In this *cache* Joan Ford waited till her daughter returned, leading the recovered man.

She would at once have bound his eyes, lest he should recognise the place by means of which access was obtained to the pixie treasure.

"Nay, mother," said Lemonday. "Why that, when we belong to each other? What is mine is his, and what is his is mine—for ever."

"Mother," said Guavas gravely, "it seemeth to me that all my days I have been in darkness and in poverty; and now, now only, have I found wealth and light, brought to me—by *her*." And he laid hold of Lemonday by the hand, drew her to him and kissed her lips. "And," added he, after a pause, "as with me, so with many another. We wander in a dark mine; we find treasure, and it availeth naught—till we find the one woman who alone can bring our wandering to an end, lead us out of darkness into light, and give the value to what we had lighted on in our former darkness, and in that darkness had thrust aside as worthless."

www.ingramcontent.com/pod-product-compliance
Lightning Source LLC
LaVergne TN
LVHW051232190726
843642LV00005B/1819